THE MYSTICS OF ISLAM

THE
MYSTICS OF ISLAM

BY

REYNOLD A. NICHOLSON

SCHOCKEN BOOKS • NEW YORK

First published by SCHOCKEN BOOKS 1975

Library of Congress Cataloging in Publication Data

Nicholson, Reynold Alleyne, 1868-1945.
   The Mystics of Islam.

   Reprint of the 1963 ed. published by Routledge &
   Kegan Paul, London, of a work first published in 1914.
   Bibliography: p.
   1. Sufism. I. Title.
BP189.N49 1975   297'.4   75-10713

Manufactured in the United States of America

CONTENTS

THE MYSTICS OF ISLAM

INTRODUCTION

THE title of this book sufficiently explains why it is included in a Series 'exemplifying the adventures and labours of individual seekers or groups of seekers in quest of reality.' Sūfism, the religious philosophy of Islam, is described in the oldest extant definition as 'the apprehension of divine realities,' and Mohammedan mystics are fond of calling themselves *Ahl al-Haqq*, 'the followers of the Real.'[1] In attempting to set forth their central doctrines from this point of view, I shall draw to some extent on materials which I have collected during the last twenty years for a general history of Islamic mysticism—a subject so vast and many-sided that several large volumes would be required to do it anything like justice. Here I can only sketch

---

[1] *Al-Haqq* is the term generally used by Sūfīs when they refer to God.

in broad outline certain principles, methods, and characteristic features of the inner life as it has been lived by Moslems of every class and condition from the eighth century of our era to the present day. Difficult are the paths which they threaded, dark and bewildering the pathless heights beyond; but even if we may not hope to accompany the travellers to their journey's end, any information that we have gathered concerning their religious environment and spiritual history will help us to understand the strange experiences of which they write.

In the first place, therefore, I propose to offer a few remarks on the origin and historical development of Sūfism, its relation to Islam, and its general character. Not only are these matters interesting to the student of comparative religion; some knowledge of them is indispensable to any serious student of Sūfism itself. It may be said, truly enough, that all mystical experiences ultimately meet in a single point; but that point assumes widely different aspects according to the mystic's religion, race, and temperament, while the converging lines of approach admit of almost infinite variety. Though all the great types of mysticism have something in common, each is marked by peculiar characteristics resulting from the circumstances in which it arose and flourished. Just as the Christian type cannot be understood without reference to Christianity, so the Mohammedan type must be viewed in connexion with the outward and inward development of Islam.

The word 'mystic,' which has passed from Greek religion into European literature, is represented in Arabic, Persian, and Turkish, the three chief languages of Islam, by 'Sūfī.' The terms, however, are not precisely synonymous, for 'Sūfī' has a specific religious connotation, and is restricted by usage to those mystics who profess the Mohammedan faith. And the Arabic word, although in course of time it appropriated the high significance of the Greek—lips sealed by holy mysteries, eyes closed in visionary rapture—bore a humbler meaning when it first gained currency (about 800 A.D.). Until recently its derivation was in dispute. Most Sūfīs, flying in the face of etymology, have derived it from an Arabic root which conveys the notion of 'purity'; this would make 'Sūfī' mean 'one who is pure in heart' or 'one of the elect.' Some European scholars identified it with σοφός in the sense of 'theosophist.' But Nöldeke, in an article written twenty years ago, showed conclusively that the name was derived from *sūf* (wool), and was originally applied to those Moslem ascetics who, in imitation of Christian hermits, clad themselves in coarse woollen garb as a sign of penitence and renunciation of worldly vanities.

The earliest Sūfīs were, in fact, ascetics and quietists rather than mystics. An overwhelming consciousness of sin, combined with a dread—which it is hard for us to realise—of Judgment Day and the torments of Hell-fire, so vividly painted in the Koran, drove them to seek salvation in flight from the world. On the other hand, the Koran warned them that salvation depended entirely on the inscrutable will of Allah, who guides aright the good and leads astray the wicked. Their fate was inscribed on the eternal tables of His providence, nothing could alter it. Only this was sure, that if they were destined to be saved by fasting and praying and pious works—then they would be saved. Such a belief ends naturally in quietism, complete and unquestioning submission to the divine will, an attitude characteristic of Sūfism in its oldest form. The mainspring of Moslem religious life during the eighth century was fear—fear of God, fear of Hell, fear of death, fear of sin—but the opposite motive had already begun to make its influence felt, and produced in the saintly woman Rābi'a at least one conspicuous example of truly mystical self-abandonment.

So far, there was no great difference
between the Sūfī and the orthodox Mohammedan zealot, except that the Sūfīs attached
extraordinary importance to certain Koranic
doctrines, and developed them at the
expense of others which many Moslems
might consider equally essential. It must
also be allowed that the ascetic movement
was inspired by Christian ideals, and con-
trasted sharply with the active and pleasure-
loving spirit of Islam. In a famous sentence
the Prophet denounced monkish austerities
and bade his people devote themselves to
the holy war against unbelievers; and he
gave, as is well known, the most convincing
testimony in favour of marriage. Although
his condemnation of celibacy did not remain without effect, the conquest of Persia,
Syria, and Egypt by his successors brought
the Moslems into contact with ideas which
profoundly modified their outlook on life
and religion. European readers of the
Koran cannot fail to be struck by its
author's vacillation and inconsistency in
dealing with the greatest problems. He
himself was not aware of these contradictions, nor were they a stumbling-block to
his devout followers, whose simple faith
accepted the Koran as the Word of God.
But the rift was there, and soon produced
far-reaching results.

Hence arose the Murjites, who set faith

above works and emphasised the divine love
and goodness; the Qadarites who affirmed,
and the Jabarites who denied, that men are
responsible for their actions; the Mu'tazilites,
who built a theology on the basis of reason,
rejecting the qualities of Allah as incompatible with His unity, and predestinarian-
ism as contrary to His justice; and finally
the Ash'arites, the scholastic theologians
of Islam, who formulated the rigid metaphysical and doctrinal system that underlies
the creed of orthodox Mohammedans at the
present time. All these speculations, influenced as they were by Greek theology
and philosophy, reacted powerfully upon
Sūfism. Early in the third century of the
Hegira—the ninth after Christ—we find
manifest signs of the new leaven stirring
within it. Not that Sūfīs ceased to mortify
the flesh and take pride in their poverty,
but they now began to regard asceticism as
only the first stage of a long journey, the
preliminary training for a larger spiritual
life than the mere ascetic is able to conceive.
The nature of the change may be illustrated
by quoting a few sentences which have come
down to us from the mystics of this period.

    " Love is not to be learned from
men: it is one of God's gifts and
comes of His grace."

    " None refrains from the lusts of this
world save him in whose heart there is a

light that keeps him always busied with
the next world."

" When the gnostic's spiritual eye is
opened, his bodily eye is shut : he sees
nothing but God."

" If gnosis were to take visible shape
all who looked thereon would die at the
sight of its beauty and loveliness and
goodness and grace, and every bright-
ness would become dark beside the
splendour thereof." [1]

" Gnosis is nearer to silence than to
speech."

" When the heart weeps because it
has lost, the spirit laughs because it has
found."

" Nothing sees God and dies, even as
nothing sees God and lives, because His
life is everlasting : whoever sees it is
thereby made everlasting."

" O God, I never listen to the cry of
animals or to the quivering of trees or
to the murmuring of water or to the
warbling of birds or to the rustling
wind or to the crashing thunder without feeling them to be an evidence of
Thy unity and a proof that there is
nothing like unto Thee."

---

[1] Compare Plato, *Phædrus* (Jowett's translation): " For
sight is the keenest of our bodily senses ; though not by
that is wisdom seen ; her loveliness would have been trans-
porting if there had been a visible image of her."

" O my God, I invoke Thee in public
as lords are invoked, but in private as
loved ones are invoked.   Publicly I say,
'O my God!' but privately I say, 'O
my Beloved!'"

These ideas—Light, Knowledge, and Love
—form, as it were, the keynotes of the new
Sūfism, and in the following chapters I shall
endeavour to show how they were developed.
Ultimately they rest upon a pantheistic
faith which deposed the One transcendent
God of Islam and worshipped in His stead
One Real Being who dwells and works
everywhere, and whose throne is not less,
but more, in the human heart than in the
heaven of heavens.   Before going further, it
will be convenient to answer a question
which the reader may have asked himself—
Whence did the Moslems of the ninth century
derive this doctrine ?

Modern research has proved that the
origin of Sūfism cannot be traced back to
a single definite cause, and has thereby
discredited the sweeping generalisations
which represent it, for instance, as a reaction
of the Aryan mind against a conquering
Semitic religion, and as the product, essentially, of Indian or Persian thought.   State-
ments of this kind, even when they are
partially true, ignore the principle that
in order to establish an historical connexion
between A and B, it is not enough to bring

forward evidence of their likeness to one
another, without showing at the same time
(1) that the actual relation of B to A was
such as to render the assumed filiation
possible, and (2) that the possible hypothesis
fits in with all the ascertained and relevant
facts. Now, the theories which I have
mentioned do not satisfy these conditions.
If Sūfism was nothing but a revolt of the
Aryan spirit, how are we to explain the
undoubted fact that some of the leading
pioneers of Mohammedan mysticism were
natives of Syria and Egypt, and Arabs by
race ? Similarly, the advocates of a Buddhistic or Vedāntic origin forget that the
main current of Indian influence upon
Islamic civilisation belongs to a later epoch,
whereas Moslem theology, philosophy, and
science put forth their first luxuriant shoots
on a soil that was saturated with Hellenistic
culture. The truth is that Sūfism is a
complex thing, and therefore no simple
answer can be given to the question how
it originated. We shall have gone far,
however, towards answering that question
when we have distinguished the various
movements and forces which moulded
Sūfism, and determined what direction it
should take in the early stages of its
growth.

Let us first consider the most important
external, *i.e.* non-Islamic, influences.

I. CHRISTIANITY

It is obvious that the ascetic and quietistic tendencies to which I have referred were in harmony with Christian theory and drew nourishment therefrom. Many Gospel texts and apocryphal sayings of Jesus are cited in the oldest Sūfī biographies, and the Christian anchorite (*rāhib*) often appears in the *rôle* of a teacher giving instruction and advice to wandering Moslem ascetics. We have seen that the woollen dress, from which the name ' Sūfī ' is derived, is of Christian origin : vows of silence, litanies (*dhikr*), and other ascetic practices may be traced to the same source. As regards the doctrine of divine love, the following extracts speak for themselves :

"Jesus passed by three men. Their bodies were lean and their faces pale. He asked them, saying, ' What hath brought you to this plight ? ' They answered, ' Fear of the Fire.' Jesus said, ' Ye fear a thing created, and it behoves God that He should save those who fear.' Then he left them and passed by three others, whose faces were paler and their bodies leaner, and asked them, saying, ' What hath brought you to this plight ? ' They answered, ' Longing for Paradise.' He said, ' Ye

desire a thing created, and it behoves
God that He should give you that
which ye hope for.' Then he went on
and passed by three others of exceeding
paleness and leanness, so that their
faces were as mirrors of light, and he
said, ' What hath brought you to this ? '
They answered, ' Our love of God.'
Jesus said, ' Ye are the nearest to Him,
ye are the nearest to Him.' "

The Syrian mystic, Ahmad ibn al-Hawārī,
once asked a Christian hermit :

" ' What is the strongest command
that ye find in your Scriptures ? ' The
hermit replied : ' We find none stronger
than this : " Love thy Creator with
all thy power and might." ' "

Another hermit was asked by some Moslem
ascetics :

" ' When is a man most persevering
in devotion ? ' ' When love takes possession of his heart,' was the reply ; ' for
then he hath no joy or pleasure but in
continual devotion.' "

The influence of Christianity through its
hermits, monks, and heretical sects (*e.g.* the
Messalians or Euchitæ) was twofold : ascetic
and mystical. Oriental Christian mysticism,
however, contained a Pagan element : it
had long ago absorbed the ideas and adopted
the language of Plotinus and the Neoplatonic school.

II. Neoplatonism

Aristotle, not Plato, is the dominant figure in Moslem philosophy, and few Mohammedans are familiar with the name of Plotinus, who was more commonly called 'the Greek Master' (*al-Sheykh al-Yaunānī*). But since the Arabs gained their first knowledge of Aristotle from his Neoplatonist commentators, the system with which they became imbued was that of Porphyry and Proclus.   Thus the so-called *Theology of Aristotle*, of which an Arabic version appeared in the ninth century, is actually a manual of Neoplatonism.

Another work of this school deserves particular notice : I mean the writings falsely attributed to Dionysius the Areopagite, the convert of St. Paul.   The pseudo-Dionysius —he may have been a Syrian monk—names as his teacher a certain Hierotheus, whom Frothingham has identified with Stephen Bar Sudaili, a prominent Syrian gnostic and a contemporary of Jacob of Sarūj (451–521 A.D.).   Dionysius quotes some fragments of erotic hymns by this Stephen, and a complete work, the *Book of Hierotheus on the Hidden Mysteries of the Divinity*, has come down to us in a unique manuscript which is now in the British Museum.   The Dionysian writings, turned into Latin by John Scotus Erigena, founded medieval Christian mysticism in Western Europe. Their influence in the East was hardly less vital. They were translated from Greek into Syriac almost immediately on their appearance, and their doctrine was vigorously propagated by commentaries in the same tongue. "About 850 A.D. Dionysius was known from the Tigris to the Atlantic."

Besides literary tradition, there were other channels by which the doctrines of emanation, illumination, gnosis, and ecstasy were transmitted, but enough has been said to convince the reader that Greek mystical ideas were in the air and easily accessible to the Moslem inhabitants of Western Asia and Egypt, where the Sūfī theosophy first took shape. One of those who bore the chief part in its development, Dhu 'l-Nūn the Egyptian, is described as a philosopher and alchemist—in other words, a student of Hellenistic science. When it is added that much of his speculation agrees with what we find, for example, in the writings of Dionysius, we are drawn irresistibly to the conclusion (which, as I have pointed out, is highly probable on general grounds) that Neoplatonism poured into Islam a large tincture of the same mystical element in which Christianity was already steeped.

III. Gnosticism.[1]

Though little direct evidence is available, the conspicuous place occupied by the theory of gnosis in early Sūfī speculation suggests contact with Christian Gnosticism, and it is worth noting that the parents of Ma'rūf al-Karkhī, whose definition of Sūfism as 'the apprehension of divine realities' was quoted on the first page of this Introduction, are said to have been Sābians, *i.e.* Mandæans, dwelling in the Babylonian fenland between Basra and Wāsit. Other Moslem saints had learned 'the mystery of the Great Name.' It was communicated to Ibrāhīm ibn Adham by a man whom he met while travelling in the desert, and as soon as he pronounced it he saw the prophet Khadir (Elias). The ancient Sūfīs borrowed from the Manichæans the term *siddīq*, which they apply to their own spiritual adepts, and a later school, returning to the dualism of Mānī, held the view that the diversity of phenomena arises from the admixture of light and darkness.

> "The ideal of human action is freedom from the taint of darkness; and the freedom of light from darkness

[1] Cf. Goldziher, "Neuplatonische und gnostische Elemente im Hadīt," in *Zeitschrift für Assyriologie*, xxii. 317 ff.

means the self-consciousness of light as light." [1]

The following version of the doctrine of the seventy thousand veils as explained by a modern Rifā'ī dervish shows clear traces of Gnosticism and is so interesting that I cannot refrain from quoting it here:

" Seventy Thousand Veils separate Allah, the One Reality, from the world of matter and of sense. And every soul passes before his birth through these seventy thousand. The inner half of these are veils of light: the outer half, veils of darkness. For every one of the veils of light passed through, in this journey towards birth, the soul puts *off* a divine quality: and for every one of the dark veils, it puts *on* an earthly quality. Thus the child is born *weeping*, for the soul knows its separation from Allah, the One Reality. And when the child cries in its sleep, it is because the soul remembers something of what it has lost. Otherwise, the passage through the veils has brought with it forgetfulness (*nisyān*): and for this reason man is called *insān*. He is now, as it were, in prison in his body, separated by these thick curtains from Allah.

[1] Shaikh Muhammad Iqbal, *The Development of Metaphysics in Persia* (1908), p. 150.

" But the whole purpose of Sūfism, the Way of the dervish, is to give him an escape from this prison, an apocalypse of the Seventy Thousand Veils, a recovery of the original unity with The One, *while still in this body*. The body is not to be put off ; it is to be refined and made spiritual—a help and not a hindrance to the spirit. It is like a metal that has to be refined by fire and transmuted. And the sheikh tells the aspirant that he has the secret of this transmutation. ' We shall throw you into the fire of Spiritual Passion,' he says, ' and you will emerge refined.' " [1]

IV. BUDDHISM

Before the Mohammedan conquest of India in the eleventh century, the teaching of Buddha exerted considerable influence in Eastern Persia and Transoxania. We hear of flourishing Buddhist monasteries in Balkh, the metropolis of ancient Bactria, a city famous for the number of Sūfīs who resided in it. Professor Goldziher has called attention to the significant circumstance that the Sūfī ascetic, Ibrāhīm ibn Adham, appears in Moslem legend as a prince of Balkh who abandoned his throne and

[1] *"The Way"* of a Mohammedan Mystic, by W. H. T. Gairdner (Leipzig, 1912), pp. 9 f.

became a wandering dervish—the story of Buddha over again. The Sūfīs learned the use of rosaries from Buddhist monks, and, without entering into details, it may be safely asserted that the method of Sūfism, so far as it is one of ethical self-culture, ascetic meditation, and intellectual abstraction, owes a good deal to Buddhism. But the features which the two systems have in common only accentuate the fundamental difference between them. In spirit they are poles apart. The Buddhist moralises himself, the Sūfī becomes moral only through knowing and loving God.

The Sūfī conception of the passing-away (*fanā*) of individual self in Universal Being is certainly, I think, of Indian origin. Its first great exponent was the Persian mystic, Bāyazīd of Bistām, who may have received it from his teacher, Abū 'Alī of Sind (Scinde). Here are some of his sayings :

"Creatures are subject to changing 'states,' but the gnostic has no 'state,' because his vestiges are effaced and his essence annihilated by the essence of another, and his traces are lost in another's traces."

"Thirty years the high God was my mirror, now I am my own mirror," *i.e.* according to the explanation given by his biographer, "that which I was I am no more, for 'I' and 'God' is a denial

of the unity of God. Since I am no
more, the high God is His own mirror."
   " I went from God to God, until they
cried from me in me, ' O Thou I ! ' "

This, it will be observed, is not Buddhism,
but the pantheism of the Vedānta. We
cannot identify *fanā* with Nirvāṇa uncon-
ditionally. Both terms imply the passing-
away of individuality, but while Nirvāna
is purely negative, *fanā* is accompanied by
baqā, everlasting life in God. The rapture
of the Sūfī who has lost himself in ecstatic
contemplation of the divine beauty is
entirely opposed to the passionless intellectual serenity of the Arahat. I emphasise
this contrast because, in my opinion, the
influence of Buddhism on Mohammedan
thought has been exaggerated. Much is
attributed to Buddhism that is Indian
rather than specifically Buddhistic : the *fanā*
theory of the Sūfīs is a case in point.
Ordinary Moslems held the followers of
Buddha in abhorrence, regarding them as
idolaters, and were not likely to seek personal intercourse with them. On the other
hand, for nearly a thousand years before
the Mohammedan conquest, Buddhism had
been powerful in Bactria and Eastern Persia
generally : it must, therefore, have affected
the development of Sūfism in these regions.
   While *fanā* in its pantheistic form is

radically different from Nirvāṇa, the terms
coincide so closely in other ways that we
cannot regard them as being altogether
unconnected. *Fanā* has an ethical aspect :
it involves the extinction of all passions and
desires. The passing-away of evil qualities
and of the evil actions which they produce
is said to be brought about by the continuance of the corresponding good qualities
and actions. Compare this with the definition
of Nirvāna given by Professor Rhys Davids :

> " The extinction of that sinful, grasp-
> ing condition of mind and heart, which
> would otherwise, according to the great
> mystery of Karma, be the cause of
> renewed individual existence. That
> extinction is to be brought about by,
> and runs parallel with, the growth of
> the opposite condition of mind and
> heart ; and it is complete when that
> opposite condition is reached."

Apart from the doctrine of Karma, which
is alien to Sūfism, these definitions of *fanā*
(viewed as a moral state) and Nirvāṇa
agree almost word for word. It would be
out of place to pursue the comparison
further, but I think we may conclude that
the Sūfī theory of *fanā* was influenced to
some extent by Buddhism as well as by
Perso-Indian pantheism.

The receptivity of Islam to foreign ideas
has been recognised by every unbiassed

inquirer, and the history of Sūfism is only a single instance of the general rule. But this fact should not lead us to seek in such ideas an explanation of the whole question which I am now discussing, or to identify Sūfism itself with the extraneous ingredients which it absorbed and assimilated in the course of its development. Even if Islam had been miraculously shut off from contact with foreign religions and philosophies, some form of mysticism would have arisen within it, for the seeds were already there. Of course, we cannot isolate the internal forces working in this direction, since they were subject to the law of spiritual gravitation. The powerful currents of thought discharged through the Mohammedan world by the great non-Islamic systems above mentioned gave a stimulus to various tendencies within Islam which affected Sūfism either positively or negatively. As we have seen, its oldest type is an ascetic revolt against luxury and worldliness ; later on, the prevailing rationalism and scepticism provoked counter-movements towards intuitive knowledge and emotional faith, and also an orthodox reaction which in its turn drove many earnest Moslems into the ranks of the mystics.

How, it may be asked, could a religion founded on the simple and austere monotheism of Mohammed tolerate these new

doctrines, much less make terms with them ?
It would seem impossible to reconcile the
transcendent personality of Allah with an
immanent Reality which is the very life
and soul of the universe. Yet Islam has
accepted Sūfism. The Sūfīs, instead of being
excommunicated, are securely established
in the Mohammedan church, and the *Legend
of the Moslem Saints* records the wildest
excesses of Oriental pantheism.

Let us return for a moment to the Koran,
that infallible touchstone by which every
Mohammedan theory and practice must be
proved. Are any germs of mysticism to
be found there ? The Koran, as I have
said, starts with the notion of Allah, the
One, Eternal, and Almighty God, far above
human feelings and aspirations—the Lord
of His slaves, not the Father of His children ;
a judge meting out stern justice to sinners,
and extending His mercy only to those who
avert His wrath by repentance, humility,
and unceasing works of devotion; a God
of fear rather than of love. This is one
side, and certainly the most prominent side,
of Mohammed's teaching; but while he
set an impassable gulf between the world
and Allah, his deeper instinct craved a
direct revelation from God to the soul.
There are no contradictions in the logic of
feeling. Mohammed, who had in him something of the mystic, felt God both as far and

near, both as transcendent and immanent.
In the latter aspect, Allah is the light
of the heavens and the earth, a Being who
works in the world and in the soul of man.

> " If My servants ask thee about Me,
> lo, I am near " (Kor. 2. 182); " We
> (God) are nearer to him than his own
> neck-vein " (50. 15); " And in the
> earth are signs to those of real faith,
> and in yourselves. What! do ye not
> see ? " (51. 20–21).

It was a long time ere they saw. The
Moslem consciousness, haunted by terrible
visions of the wrath to come, slowly and
painfully awoke to the significance of those
liberating ideas.

The verses which I have quoted do not
stand alone, and however unfavourable to
mysticism the Koran as a whole may be,
I cannot assent to the view that it supplies
no basis for a mystical interpretation of
Islam. This was worked out in detail by
the Sūfīs, who dealt with the Koran in very
much the same way as Philo treated the
Pentateuch. But they would not have
succeeded so thoroughly in bringing over
the mass of religious Moslems to their side,
unless the champions of orthodoxy had set
about constructing a system of scholastic
philosophy that reduced the divine nature
to a purely formal, changeless, and absolute
unity, a bare will devoid of all affections

and emotions, a tremendous and incalculable power with which no human creature could have any communion or personal intercourse whatsoever. That is the God of Mohammedan theology. That was the alternative to Sūfism. Therefore, " all thinking, religious Moslems are mystics," as Professor D. B. Macdonald, one of our best authorities on the subject, has remarked. And he adds : " All, too, are pantheists, but some do not know it."

The relation of individual Sūfīs to Islam varies from more or less entire conformity to a merely nominal profession of belief in Allah and His Prophet. While the Koran and the Traditions are generally acknowledged to be the unalterable standard of religious truth, this acknowledgment does not include the recognition of any external authority which shall decide what is orthodox and what is heretical. Creeds and catechisms count for nothing in the Sūfī's estimation. Why should he concern himself with these when he possesses a doctrine derived immediately from God ? As he reads the Koran with studious meditation and rapt attention, lo, the hidden meanings —infinite, inexhaustible—of the Holy Word flash upon his inward eye. This is what the Sūfīs call *istinbāt*, a sort of intuitive deduction ; the mysterious inflow of divinely revealed knowledge into hearts made pure

by repentance and filled with the thought
of God, and the outflow of that knowledge
upon the interpreting tongue. Naturally,
the doctrines elicited by means of *istinbāt*
do not agree very well either with Mohammedan theology or with each other, but
the discord is easily explained. Theologians,
who interpret the letter, cannot be expected
to reach the same conclusions as mystics,
who interpret the spirit; and if both
classes differ amongst themselves, that is
a merciful dispensation of divine wisdom,
since theological controversy serves to ex-
tinguish religious error, while the variety
of mystical truth corresponds to the
manifold degrees and modes of mystical
experience.

In the chapter on the gnosis I shall enter
more fully into the attitude of the Sūfīs
towards positive religion. It is only a
rough-and-ready account of the matter to
say that many of them have been good
Moslems, many scarcely Moslems at all,
and a third party, perhaps the largest,
Moslems after a fashion. During the early
Middle Ages Islam was a growing organism,
and gradually became transformed under
the influence of diverse movements, of
which Sūfism itself was one. Mohammedan
orthodoxy in its present shape owes much
to Ghazālī, and Ghazālī was a Sūfī. Through
his work and example the Sūfistic inter-

pretation of Islam has in no small measure been harmonised with the rival claims of reason and tradition, but just because of this he is less valuable than mystics of a purer type to the student who wishes to know what Sūfism essentially is.

Although the numerous definitions of Sūfism which occur in Arabic and Persian books on the subject are historically interesting, their chief importance lies in showing that Sūfism is undefinable. Jalāluddīn Rūmī in his *Masnavī* tells a story about an elephant which some Hindoos were exhibiting in a dark room. Many people gathered to see it, but, as the place was too dark to permit them to see the elephant, they all felt it with their hands, to gain an idea of what it was like. One felt its trunk, and said that the animal resembled a water-pipe ; another felt its ear, and said it must be a large fan ; another its leg, and thought it must be a pillar ; another felt its back, and declared that the beast must be like an immense throne. So it is with those who define Sūfism : they can only attempt to express what they themselves have felt, and there is no conceivable formula that will comprise every shade of personal and intimate religious feeling. Since, however, these definitions illustrate with convenient brevity certain aspects and characteristics of Sūfism, a few specimens may be given.

" Sūfism is this : that actions should be passing over the Sūfī (*i.e.* being done upon him) which are known to God only, and that he should always be with God in a way that is known to God only."

" Sūfism is wholly self-discipline."

" Sūfism is, to possess nothing and to be possessed by nothing."

" Sūfism is not a system composed of rules or sciences but a moral disposition ; *i.e.* if it were a rule, it could be made one's own by strenuous exertion, and if it were a science, it could be acquired by instruction ; but on the contrary it is a disposition, according to the saying, ' Form yourselves on the moral nature of God ' ; and the moral nature of God cannot be attained either by means of rules or by means of sciences."

" Sūfism is freedom and generosity and absence of self-constraint."

" It is this : that God should make thee die to thyself and should make thee live in Him."

" To behold the imperfection of the phenomenal world, nay, to close the eye to everything imperfect in contemplation of Him who is remote from all imperfection—that is Sūfism."

" Sūfism is control of the faculties and observance of the breaths."

" It is Sūfism to put away what thou hast in thy head, to give what thou hast in thy hand, and not to recoil from whatsoever befalls thee."

The reader will perceive that Sūfism is a word uniting many divergent meanings, and that in sketching its main features one is obliged to make a sort of composite portrait, which does not represent any particular type exclusively. The Sūfīs are not a sect, they have no dogmatic system, the *tarīqas* or paths by which they seek God " are in number as the souls of men " and vary infinitely, though a family likeness may be traced in them all. Descriptions of such a Protean phenomenon must differ widely from one another, and the impression produced in each case will depend on the choice of materials and the prominence given to this or that aspect of the many-sided whole. Now, the essence of Sūfism is best displayed in its extreme type, which is pantheistic and speculative rather than ascetic or devotional. This type, therefore, I have purposely placed in the foreground. The advantage of limiting the field is obvious enough, but entails some loss of proportion. In order to form a fair judgment of Mohammedan mysticism, the following chapters should be supplemented by a companion picture drawn especially from those moderate types which, for want of space, I have unduly neglected,

CHAPTER I

THE PATH

MYSTICS of every race and creed have
described the progress of the spiritual life as
a journey or a pilgrimage. Other symbols
have been used for the same purpose, but
this one appears to be almost universal in
its range. The Ṣūfī who sets out to seek
God calls himself a 'traveller' (*sālik*); he
advances by slow 'stages' (*maqāmāt*) along
a 'path' (*tarīqat*) to the goal of union with
Reality (*fanā fī 'l-Haqq*). Should he venture to make a map of this interior ascent,
it will not correspond exactly with any of
those made by previous explorers. Such
maps or scales of perfection were elaborated
by Ṣūfī teachers at an early period, and the
unlucky Moslem habit of systematising has
produced an enormous aftercrop. The
'path' expounded by the author of the *Kitāb
al-Lumaʿ*, perhaps the oldest comprehensive
treatise on Ṣūfism that we now possess,
consists of the following seven 'stages,' each
of which (except the first member of the series)
is the result of the 'stages' immediately

preceding it—(1) Repentance, (2) abstinence, (3) renunciation, (4) poverty, (5) patience, (6) trust in God, (7) satisfaction. The 'stages' constitute the *ascetic and ethical* discipline of the Sūfī, and must be carefully distinguished from the so-called 'states' (*ahwāl*, plural of *hāl*), which form a similar *psychological* chain. The writer whom I have just quoted enumerates ten 'states'—Meditation, nearness to God, love, fear, hope, longing, intimacy, tranquillity, contemplation, and certainty. While the 'stages' can be acquired and mastered by one's own efforts, the 'states' are spiritual feelings and dispositions over which a man has no control:

> "They descend from God into his heart, without his being able to repel them when they come or to retain them when they go."

The Sūfī's 'path' is not finished until he has traversed all the 'stages,' making himself perfect in every one of them before advancing to the next, and has also experienced whatever 'states' it pleases God to bestow upon him. Then, and only then, is he permanently raised to the higher planes of consciousness which Sūfīs call 'the Gnosis' (*ma'rifat*) and 'the Truth' (*haqīqat*), where the 'seeker' (*tālib*) becomes the 'knower' or 'gnostic' (*'ārif*), and realises that knowledge, knower, and known are One.

Having sketched, as briefly as possible, the external framework of the method by which the Súfí approaches his goal, I shall now try to give some account of its inner workings. The present chapter deals with the first portion of the threefold journey—the Path, the Gnosis, and the Truth—by which the quest of Reality is often symbolised.

The first place in every list of ' stages ' is occupied by repentance (*tawbat*). This is the Moslem term for ' conversion,' and marks the beginning of a new life. In the biographies of eminent Súfís the dreams, visions, auditions, and other experiences which caused them to enter on the Path are usually related. Trivial as they may seem, these records have a psychological basis, and, if authentic, would be worth studying in detail. Repentance is described as the awakening of the soul from the **Repentance.** slumber of heedlessness, so that the sinner becomes aware of his evil ways and feels contrition for past disobedience. He is not truly penitent, however, unless (1) he at once abandons the sin or sins of which he is conscious, and (2) firmly resolves that he will never return to these sins in the future. It he should fail to keep his vow, he must again turn to God, whose mercy is infinite. A certain well-known Súfí repented seventy times and fell back into sin seventy times before he made a

lasting repentance. The convert must also,
as far as lies in his power, satisfy all those
whom he has injured. Many examples of
such restitution might be culled from the
Legend of the Moslem Saints.

According to the high mystical theory,
repentance is purely an act of divine grace,
coming from God to man, not from man to
God. Some one said to Rābi'a :

> " I have committed many sins ; if
> I turn in penitence towards God, will
> He turn in mercy towards me ? "
> " Nay," she replied, " but if He shall
> turn towards thee, thou wilt turn
> towards Him."

The question whether sins ought to be
remembered after repentance or forgotten
illustrates a fundamental point in Sūfī
ethics : I mean the difference between what
is taught to novices and disciples and what
is held as an esoteric doctrine by adepts.
Any Mohammedan director of souls would
tell his pupils that to think humbly and
remorsefully of one's sins is a sovereign
remedy against spiritual pride, but he himself might very well believe that real repentance consists in forgetting everything
except God.

> " The penitent," says Hujwīrī, " is
> a lover of God, and the lover of God
> is in contemplation of God : in con-
> templation it is wrong to remember

sin, for recollection of sin is a veil
between God and the contemplative."
Sin appertains to self-existence, which
itself is the greatest of all sins.   To forget
sin is to forget self.

This is only one application of a principle
which, as I have said, runs through the
whole ethical system of Sūfism and will be
more fully explained in a subsequent chapter.
Its dangers are evident, but we must in
fairness allow that the same theory of conduct may not be equally suitable to those
who have made themselves perfect in moral
discipline and to those who are still striving
after perfection.

Over the gate of repentance it is written:

" All *self* abandon ye who enter here!"

The convert now begins what is called by
Christian mystics the Purgative Way.   If
he follows the general rule, he will take a
director (Sheykh, Pīr, Murshid), *i.e.* a holy
man of ripe experience and pro-
found knowledge, whose least
word is absolute law to his disciples.   A
' seeker ' who attempts to traverse the
' Path ' without assistance receives little
sympathy.   Of such a one it is said that ' his
guide is Satan,' and he is likened to a tree
that for want of the gardener's care brings
forth ' none or bitter fruit.'   Speaking of
the Sūfī Sheykhs, Hujwīrī says :

The Sheykh.

" When a novice joins them, with
the purpose of renouncing the world,
they subject him to spiritual discipline
for the space of three years. If he
fulfil the requirements of this discipline,
well and good ; otherwise, they declare
that he cannot be admitted to the
' Path.' The first year is devoted to
service of the people, the second year
to service of God, and the third year to
watching over his own heart. He can
serve the people, only when he places
himself in the rank of servants and all
others in the rank of masters, *i.e.* he
must regard all, without exception, as
being better than himself, and must
deem it his duty to serve all alike. And
he can serve God, only when he cuts
off all his selfish interests relating either
to the present or to the future life, and
worships God for God's sake alone,
inasmuch as whoever worships God for
any thing's sake worships himself, not
God. And he can watch over his heart,
only when his thoughts are collected
and every care is dismissed, so that in
communion with God he guards his
heart from the assaults of heedlessness. When these qualifications are
possessed by the novice, he may
wear the *muraqqa'at* (the patched
frock worn by dervishes) as a true

mystic, not merely as an imitator of
others."

Shiblī was a pupil of the famous theosophist Junayd of Baghdād. On his conversion, he came to Junayd, saying :

" They tell me that you possess the
pearl of divine knowledge : either give
it me or sell it." Junayd answered :
" I cannot sell it, for you have not the
price thereof ; and if I give it you, you
will have gained it cheaply. You do
not know its value. Cast yourself head-
long, like me, into this ocean, in order
that you may win the pearl by waiting
patiently."

Shiblī asked what he must do.

" Go," said Junayd, " and sell
sulphur."

At the end of a year he said to Shiblī :

" This trading makes you well known.
Become a dervish and occupy yourself
solely with begging."

During a whole year Shiblī wandered
through the streets of Baghdād, begging of
the passers-by, but no one heeded him.
Then he returned to Junayd, who exclaimed :

" See now ! You are nothing in
people's eyes. Never set your mind on
them or take any account of them at
all. For some time " (he continued)
" you were a chamberlain and acted as

governor of a province. Go to that country and ask pardon of all those whom you have wronged."

Shiblī obeyed and spent four years in going from door to door, until he had obtained an acquittance from every person except one, whom he failed to trace. On his return, Junayd said to him :

"You still have some regard to reputation. Go and be a beggar for one year more."

Every day Shiblī used to bring the alms that were given him to Junayd, who bestowed them on the poor and kept Shiblī without food until the next morning. When a year had passed in this way, Junayd accepted him as one of his disciples on condition that he should perform the duties of a servant to the others. After a year's service, Junayd asked him :

"What think you of yourself now ? "
Shiblī replied : "I deem myself the meanest of God's creatures." "Now," said the master, "your faith is firm."

I need not dwell on the details of this training—the fasts and vigils, the vows of silence, the long days and nights of solitary meditation, all the weapons and tactics, in short, of that battle against one's self which the Prophet declared to be more painful and meritorious than the Holy War. On the other hand, my readers will expect me to

describe in a general way the characteristic
theories and practices for which the ' Path '
is a convenient designation. These may be
treated under the following heads : Poverty,
Mortification, Trust in God, and Recollection.
Whereas poverty is negative in nature, in-
volving detachment from all that is worldly
and unreal, the three remaining terms de-
note the positive counterpart of that process, namely, the ethical discipline by which
the soul is brought into harmonious relations
with Reality.

The fatalistic spirit which brooded darkly
over the childhood of Islam—the feeling
that all human actions are determined by
an unseen Power, and in themselves are
worthless and vain—caused renunciation to
become the watchword of early Moslem
asceticism. Every true believer is bound
to abstain from unlawful pleasures, but the
ascetic acquires merit by abstaining from
those which are lawful. At first, renunciation was understood almost exclusively in a
material sense. To have as few
Poverty. worldly goods as possible seemed
the surest means of gaining salvation.
Dāwud al-Tā'ī owned nothing except a mat
of rushes, a brick which he used as a pillow,
and a leathern vessel which served him
for drinking and washing. A certain man
dreamed that he saw Mālik ibn Dīnār and
Mohammed ibn Wāsi' being led into Para-

dise, and that Mālik was admitted before his companion. He cried out in astonishment, for he thought Mohammed ibn Wāsi' had a superior claim to the honour. "Yes," came the answer, "but Mohammed ibn Wāsi' possessed two shirts, and Mālik only one. That is the reason why Mālik is preferred."

The Sūfī ideal of poverty goes far beyond this. True poverty is not merely lack of wealth, but lack of desire for wealth : the empty heart as well as the empty hand. The 'poor man' (faqīr) and the 'mendicant' (dervīsh) are names by which the Mohammedan mystic is proud to be known, because they imply that he is stripped of every thought or wish that would divert his mind from God. "To be severed entirely from both the present life and the future life, and to want nothing besides the Lord of the present life and the future life—that is to be truly poor." Such a faqīr is denuded of individual existence, so that he does not attribute to himself any action, feeling, or quality. He may even be rich, in the common meaning of the word, though spiritually he is the poorest of the poor ; for, sometimes, God endows His saints with an outward show of wealth and worldliness in order to hide them from the profane.

No one familiar with the mystical writers will need to be informed that their terminology is ambiguous, and that the same word

frequently covers a group, if not a multi-
tude, of significations diverging more or less
widely according to the aspect from which
it is viewed. Hence the confusion that
is apparent in Sūfī text-books. When
'poverty,' for example, is explained by one
interpreter as a transcendental theory and
by another as a practical rule of religious
life, the meanings cannot coincide. Regarded from the latter standpoint, poverty
is only the beginning of Sūfism. *Faqīrs*,
Jāmī says, renounce all worldly things for
the sake of pleasing God. They are urged
to this sacrifice by one of three motives :
(*a*) Hope of an easy reckoning on the Day
of Judgment, or fear of being punished ;
(*b*) desire of Paradise ; (*c*) longing for
spiritual peace and inward composure.
Thus, inasmuch as they are not disinterested
but seek to benefit themselves, they rank
below the Sūfī, who has no will of his own
and depends absolutely on the will of God.
It is the absence of 'self' that distinguishes
the Sūfī from the *faqīr*.

Here are some maxims for dervishes :

"Do not beg unless you are starving.
The Caliph Omar flogged a man who
begged after having satisfied his hunger.
When compelled to beg, do not accept
more than you need."

"Be good-natured and uncomplain-
ing and thank God for your poverty."

" Do not flatter the rich for giving, nor blame them for withholding."

" Dread the loss of poverty more than the rich man dreads the loss of wealth."

" Take what is voluntarily offered : it is the daily bread which God sends to you : do not refuse God's gift."

" Let no thought of the morrow enter your mind, else you will incur ever-lasting perdition."

" Do not make God a springe to catch alms."

The Sūfī teachers gradually built up a system of asceticism and moral culture which is founded on the fact that there is in man an element of evil—the lower or ap-petitive soul. This evil self, the seat of passion and lust, is called *nafs* ; it may be considered broadly equivalent to 'the flesh,' and with its allies, the world and the devil, it constitutes the great obstacle to the attainment of union with God. The Prophet said : " Thy worst enemy is thy *nafs*, which is between thy two sides." I do not intend to discuss the various opinions as to its nature, but the proof of its materiality is too curious to be omitted. Mohammed ibn 'Ulyān, an eminent Sūfī, relates that one day some-thing like a young fox came forth from his throat, and God caused him to know that

it was his *nafs*. He trod on it, but it grew
bigger at every kick that he gave it. He said :

"Other things are destroyed by pain
and blows : why dost thou increase ? "
"Because I was created perverse," it
replied ; " what is pain to other things
is pleasure to me, and their pleasure is
my pain."

The *nafs* of Hallāj was seen running
behind him in the shape of a dog ; and
other cases are recorded in which it appeared
as a snake or a mouse.

Mortification of the *nafs* is the chief work
of devotion, and leads, directly or indirectly,
to the contemplative life. All the Sheykhs
are agreed that no disciple who neglects
this duty will ever learn the rudiments of
Sūfism. The principle of mortification is
Mortification. that the *nafs* should be weaned
from those things to which it is
accustomed, that it should be encouraged
to resist its passions, that its pride should
be broken, and that it should be brought
through suffering and tribulation to recognise the vileness of its original nature
and the impurity of its actions. Concerning
the outward methods of mortification, such
as fasting, silence, and solitude, a great deal
might be written, but we must now pass on
to the higher ethical discipline which com-
pletes the Path.

Self - mortification, as advanced Sūfīs

understand it, is a moral transmutation of
the inner man. When they say, "Die
before ye die," they do not mean to assert
that the lower self can be essentially destroyed, but that it can and should be purged
of its attributes, which are wholly evil.
These attributes—ignorance, pride, envy,
uncharitableness, etc.—are extinguished, and
replaced by the opposite qualities, when the
will is surrendered to God and when the
mind is concentrated on Him. Therefore
'dying to self' is really 'living in God.'
The mystical aspects of the doctrine thus
stated will occupy a considerable part of the
following chapters; here we are mainly
interested in its ethical import.

The Sūfī who has eradicated self-will is
said, in technical language, to have reached
the 'stages' of 'acquiescence' or 'satisfaction' (*ridā*) and 'trust in God' (*tawakkul*).

A dervish fell into the Tigris. Seeing
that he could not swim, a man on the
bank cried out, "Shall I tell some one
to bring you ashore?" "No," said the
dervish. "Then do you wish to be
drowned?" "No." "What, then, do
you wish?" The dervish replied, "God's
will be done! What have I to do with
wishing?"

'Trust in God,' in its extreme form, involves the renunciation of every personal
initiative and volition; total passivity like

that of a corpse in the hands of the washer who prepares it for burial ; perfect indiffer-
Trust in God. ence towards anything that is even remotely connected with one's self. A special class of the ancient Sūfīs took their name from this 'trust,' which they applied, so far as they were able, to matters of everyday life. For instance, they would not seek food, work for hire, practise any trade, or allow medicine to be given them when they were ill. Quietly they committed themselves to God's care, never doubting that He, to whom belong the treasures of earth and heaven, would provide for their wants, and that their allotted portion would come to them as surely as it comes to the birds, which neither sow nor reap, and to the fish in the sea, and to the child in the womb.

These principles depend ultimately on the Sūfistic theory of the divine unity, as is shown by Shaqīq of Balkh in the following passage :

" There are three things which a man is bound to practise. Whosoever neglects any one of them must needs neglect them all, and whosoever cleaves to any one of them must needs cleave to them all. Strive, therefore, to understand, and consider heedfully.

" The *first* is this, that with your mind and your tongue and your actions you declare God to be One ; and that,

having declared Him to be One, and
having declared that none benefits you
or harms you except Him, you devote
all your actions to Him alone.   If you
act a single jot of your actions for
the sake of another, your thought and
speech are corrupt, since your motive
in acting for another's sake must be
hope or fear ; and when you act from
hope or fear of other than God, who is
the lord and sustainer of all things, you
have taken to yourself another god to
honour and venerate.

   " *Secondly*, that while you speak and
act in the sincere belief that there is no
God except Him, you should trust Him
more than the world or money or uncle
or father or mother or any one on the
face of the earth.

   " *Thirdly*, when you have established
these two things, namely, sincere belief
in the unity of God and trust in Him,
it behoves you to be satisfied with
Him and not to be angry on account of
anything that vexes you.   Beware of
anger !   Let your heart be with Him
always, let it not be withdrawn from
Him for a single moment."

The ' trusting ' Sūfī has no thought
beyond the present hour.   On one occasion
Shaqīq asked those who sat listening to his
discourse :

" If God causes you to die to-day,
think ye that He will demand from you
the prayers of to-morrow ? " They
answered : " No ; how should He demand from us the prayers of a day on
which we are not alive ? " Shaqīq said :
" Even as He will not demand from
you the prayers of to-morrow, so do ye
not seek from Him the provender of
to-morrow. It may be that ye will not
live so long."

In view of the practical consequences of
attempting to live ' on trust,' it is not
surprising to read the advice given to those
who would perfectly fulfil the doctrine :
" Let them dig a grave and bury themselves." Later Sūfīs hold that active exertion for the purpose of obtaining the means
of subsistence is quite compatible with
' trust,' according to the saying of the
Prophet, " Trust in God and tie the camel's
leg." They define *tawakkul* as an habitual
state of mind, which is impaired only by
self-pleasing thoughts ; *e.g.* it was accounted
a breach of ' trust ' to think Paradise a
more desirable place than Hell.

What type of character is such a theory
likely to produce ? At the worst, a useless
drone and hypocrite preying upon his fellow-
creatures ; at the best, a harmless dervish
who remains unmoved in the midst of
sorrow, meets praise and blame with equal

indifference, and accepts insults, blows, torture, and death as mere incidents in the eternal drama of destiny. This cold morality, however, is not the highest of which Sūfism is capable. The highest morality springs from nothing but love, when self-surrender becomes self-devotion. Of that I shall have something to say in due time.

Among the positive elements in the Sūfī discipline there is one that Moslem mystics unanimously regard as the keystone of practical religion. I refer to the *dhikr*, an exercise well known to Western readers from the careful description given by Edward Lane in his *Modern Egyptians*, and by Professor D. B. Macdonald in his recently published *Aspects of Islam*. The term

Recollection. *dhikr*—' recollection ' seems to me the most appropriate equivalent in English—signifies ' mentioning,' ' remembering,' or simply ' thinking of '; in the Koran the Faithful are commanded to " remember God often," a plain act of worship without any mystical savour. But the Sūfīs made a practice of repeating the name of God or some religious formula, *e.g.* " Glory to Allah " (*subhān Allah*), " There is no god but Allah " (*lā ilāha illa 'llah*), accompanying the mechanical intonation with an intense concentration of every faculty upon the single word or phrase ; and they attach greater value to this irregular

litany, which enables them to enjoy unin-
terrupted communion with God, than to
the five services of prayer performed, at
fixed hours of the day and night, by all
Moslems.   Recollection may be either spoken
or silent, but it is best, according to the
usual opinion, that tongue and mind should
co-operate.   Sahl ibn 'Abdallah bade one
of his disciples endeavour to say "Allah!
Allah!" the whole day without intermission.
When he had acquired the habit of doing
so, Sahl instructed him to repeat the same
words during the night, until they came
forth from his lips even while he was asleep.
"Now," said he, "be silent and occupy
yourself with recollecting them."   At last
the disciple's whole being was absorbed by
the thought of Allah.   One day a log fell on
his head, and the words "Allah, Allah" were
seen written in the blood that trickled from
the wound.

Ghazālī describes the method and effects
of *dhikr* in a passage which Macdonald has
summarised as follows :

"Let him reduce his heart to a state
in which the existence of anything and
its non-existence are the same to him.
Then let him sit alone in some corner,
limiting his religious duties to what is
absolutely necessary, and not occupying
himself either with reciting the Koran
or considering its meaning or with

books of religious traditions or with
anything of the sort. And let him see
to it that nothing save God most High
enters his mind. Then, as he sits in
solitude, let him not cease saying
continuously with his tongue, ' *Allah,
Allah,*' keeping his thought on it. At
last he will reach a state when the motion
of his tongue will cease, and it will
seem as though the word flowed from
it. Let him persevere in this until all
trace of motion is removed from his
tongue, and he finds his heart persevering
in the thought. Let him still persevere
until the form of the word, its letters
and shape, is removed from his heart,
and there remains the idea alone, as
though clinging to his heart, inseparable
from it. So far, all is dependent on his
will and choice ; but to bring the mercy
of God does not stand in his will or
choice. He has now laid himself bare
to the breathings of that mercy, and
nothing remains but to await what
God will open to him, as God has done
after this manner to prophets and saints.
If he follows the above course, he may
be sure that the light of the Real will
shine out in his heart. At first unstable,
like a flash of lightning, it turns and
returns ; though sometimes it hangs
back. And if it returns, sometimes it

abides and sometimes it is momentary.
And if it abides, sometimes its abiding
is long, and sometimes short."

Another Sūfī puts the gist of the matter
in a sentence, thus :

" The first stage of *dhikr* is to forget
self, and the last stage is the effacement of the worshipper in the act of
worship, without consciousness of worship, and such absorption in the object
of worship as precludes return to the
subject thereof."

Recollection can be aided in various ways.
When Shiblī was a novice, he went daily
into a cellar, taking with him a bundle of
sticks. If his attention flagged, he would
beat himself until the sticks broke, and
sometimes the whole bundle would be
finished before evening ; then he would
dash his hands and feet against the wall.
The Indian practice of inhaling and exhaling
the breath was known to the Sūfīs of the
ninth century and was much used afterwards.
Among the Dervish Orders music, singing,
and dancing are favourite means of inducing
the state of trance called ' passing-away '
(*fanā*), which, as appears from the definition
quoted above, is the climax and *raison d'être*
of the method.

In ' meditation ' (*murāqabat*) we recognise
a form of self-concentration similar to the
Buddhistic *dhyāna* and *samādhi*. This is

what the Prophet meant when he said,
" Worship God as though thou sawest Him,
for if thou seest Him not, yet He sees thee."
Any one who feels sure that God is always
watching over him will devote himself to
Meditation. meditating on God, and no evil
thoughts or diabolic suggestions
will find their way into his heart. Nūrī
used to meditate so intently that not a hair
on his body stirred. He declared that he
had learned this habit from a cat which
was observing a mouse-hole, and that she
was far more quiet than he. Abū Saʿīd
ibn Abi ʾl-Khayr kept his eyes fixed on his
navel. It is said that the Devil is smitten
with epilepsy when he approaches a man
thus occupied, just as happens to other men
when the Devil takes possession of them.

This chapter will have served its purpose
if it has brought before my readers a clear
view of the main lines on which the pre-
paratory training of the Sūfī is conducted.
We must now imagine him to have been
invested by his Sheykh with the patched
frock (*muraqqaʿat* or *khirqat*), which is an
outward sign that he has successfully
emerged from the discipline of the ' Path,'
and is now advancing with uncertain steps
towards the Light, as when toil-worn
travellers, having gained the summit of a
deep gorge, suddenly catch glimpses of the
sun and cover their eyes.

CHAPTER II

ILLUMINATION AND ECSTASY

GOD, who is described in the Koran as "the Light of the heavens and the earth," cannot be seen by the bodily eye. He is visible only to the inward sight of the 'heart.' In the next chapter we shall return to this spiritual organ, but I am not going to enter into the intricacies of Sūfī psychology any further than is necessary. The 'vision of the heart' (*ru'yat al-qalb*) is defined as "the heart's beholding by the light of certainty that which is hidden in the unseen world." This is what 'Alī meant when he was asked, "Do you see God?" and replied: "How should we worship One whom we do not see?" The light of intuitive certainty (*yaqīn*) by which the heart sees God is a beam of God's own light cast therein by Himself; else no vision of Him were possible.

"'Tis the sun's self that lets the sun be seen."

According to a mystical interpretation of the famous passage in the Koran where the light of Allah is compared to a candle burning in a lantern of transparent glass, which is placed in a niche in the wall, the niche is the true believer's heart; therefore his speech is light and his works are light and he moves in light. " He who discourses of eternity," said Bāyazīd, "must have within him the lamp of eternity."

The light which gleams in the heart of the illuminated mystic endows him with a supernatural power of discernment (*firāsat*). Although the Sūfīs, like all other Moslems, acknowledge Mohammed to be the last of the prophets (as, from a different point of view, he is the Logos or first of created beings), they really claim to possess a minor form of inspiration. When Nūrī was questioned concerning the origin of mystical *firāsat*, he answered by quoting the Koranic verse in which God says that He breathed His spirit into Adam; but the more orthodox Sūfīs, who strenously combat the doctrine that the human spirit is uncreated and eternal, affirm that *firāsat* is the result of knowledge and insight, metaphorically called ' light ' or ' inspiration,' which God creates and bestows upon His favourites. The Tradition, " Beware of the discernment of the true believer, for he sees by the light of Allah," is exemplified in such anecdotes as these :

Abū 'Abdallah al-Rāzī said :

"Ibn al-Anbārī presented me with a

woollen frock, and seeing on the head
of Shiblī a bonnet that would just
match it, I conceived the wish that
they were both mine. When Shiblī
rose to depart, he looked at me, as he
was in the habit of doing when he
desired me to follow him. So I followed
him to his house, and when we had gone
in, he bade me put off the frock and
took it from me and folded it and threw
his bonnet on the top. Then he called
for a fire and burnt both frock and
bonnet."

Sarī al-Saqatī frequently urged Junayd
to speak in public, but Junayd was unwilling
to consent, for he doubted whether he was
worthy of such an honour. One Friday night
he dreamed that the Prophet appeared and
commanded him to speak to the people.
He awoke and went to Sarī's house before
daybreak, and knocked at the door. Sarī
opened the door and said : " You would not
believe me until the Prophet came and told
you."

Sahl ibn 'Abdallah was sitting in the congregational mosque when a pigeon, overcome
by the intense heat, dropped on the floor.
Sahl exclaimed : " Please God, Shāh al-
Kirmānī has just died." They wrote it
down, and it was found to be true.

When the heart is purged of sin and evil
thoughts, the light of certainty strikes upon

it and makes it a shining mirror, so that
the Devil cannot approach it without being observed. Hence the saying of some
gnostic : " If I disobey my heart, I disobey
God." It was a man thus illuminated to
whom the Prophet said : " Consult thy
heart, and thou wilt hear the secret ordinance
of God proclaimed by the heart's inward
knowledge, which is real faith and divinity "
—something much better than the learning
of divines. I need not anticipate here the
question, which will be discussed in the
following chapter, how far the claims of an
infallible conscience are reconcilable with
external religion and morality. The
Prophet, too, prayed that God would put a
light into his ear and into his eye ; and after
mentioning the different members of his
body, he concluded, " and make the whole
of me one light." [1] From illumination of
gradually increasing splendour, the mystic
rises to contemplation of the divine attributes, and ultimately, when his consciousness
is wholly melted away, he becomes transub-
stantiated (tajawhara) in the radiance of
the divine essence. This is the ' station '
of well-doing (ihsān)—for " God is with the
well-doers " (Kor. 29. 69), and we have

[1] The reader should be reminded that most, if not all,
mystical Traditions ascribed to Mohammed were forged
and fathered upon him by the Sūfīs, who represent themselves as the true interpreters of his esoteric teaching.

Prophetic authority for the statement that "well-doing consists in worshipping God as though thou wert seeing Him."

I will not waste the time and abuse the patience of my readers by endeavouring to classify and describe these various grades of illumination, which may be depicted symbolically but cannot be explained in scientific language. We must allow the mystics to speak for themselves. Granted that their teaching is often hard to understand, it conveys more of the truth than we can ever hope to obtain from analysis and dissection.

Here are two passages from the oldest Persian treatise on Sūfism, the *Kashf al-Mahjūb* of Hujwīrī :

"It is related that Sarī al-Saqatī said, ' O God, whatever punishment thou mayst inflict upon me, do not punish me with the humiliation of being veiled from Thee,' because, if I am not veiled from Thee, my torment and affliction will be lightened by the recollection and contemplation of Thee ; but if I am veiled from Thee, even Thy bounty will be deadly to me. There is no punishment in Hell more painful and hard to bear than that of being veiled. If God were revealed in Hell to the people of Hell, sinful believers would never think of Paradise, since

the sight of God would so fill them with
joy that they would not feel bodily
pain. And in Paradise there is no
pleasure more perfect than unveiled-
ness. If the people there enjoyed all
the pleasures of that place and other
pleasures a hundredfold, but were
veiled from God, their hearts would
be utterly broken. Therefore it is the
way of God to let the hearts of those
who love Him have vision of Him
always, in order that the delight thereof may enable them to endure every
tribulation; and they say in their
visions, ' We deem all torments more
desirable than to be veiled from Thee.
When Thy beauty is revealed to our
hearts, we take no thought of affliction.' "

" There are really two kinds of contemplation. The former is the result
of perfect faith, the latter of rapturous
love, for in the rapture of love a man
attains to such a degree that his whole
being is absorbed in the thought of
his Beloved and he sees nothing else.
Muhammad ibn Wāsi' said : ' I never
saw anything without seeing God therein,' *i.e.* through perfect faith. Shiblī
said : ' I never saw anything except
God,' *i.e.* in the rapture of love and the
fervour of contemplation. One mystic

sees the act with his bodily eye, and, as he looks, beholds the Agent with his spiritual eye ; another is rapt by love of the Agent from all things else, so that he sees only the Agent. The one method is demonstrative, the other is ecstatic. In the former case, a manifest proof is derived from the evidences of God ; in the latter case, the seer is enraptured and transported by desire : evidences are a veil to him, because he who knows a thing does not care for aught besides, and he who loves a thing does not regard aught besides, but renounces contention with God and interference with Him in His decrees and acts. When the lover turns his eye away from created things, he will inevitably see the Creator with his heart. God hath said, ' Tell the believers to close their eyes ' (Kor. 24. 30), *i.e.* to close their bodily eyes to lusts and their spiritual eyes to created things. He who is most sincere in self-mortification is most firmly grounded in contemplation. Sahl ibn 'Abdallah of Tustar said : ' If any one shuts his eye to God for a single moment, he will never be rightly guided all his life long,' because to regard other than God is to be handed over to other than God, and one who is

left at the mercy of other than God is
lost. Therefore the life of contempla-
tives is the time during which they
enjoy contemplation; time spent in
ocular vision they do not reckon as
life, for that to them is really death.
Thus, when Bāyazīd was asked how
old he was, he replied, ' Four years.'
They said to him, ' How can that be ? '
He answered, ' I have been veiled from
God by this world for seventy years,
but I have seen Him during the last
four years : the period in which one is
veiled does not belong to one's life.' "
I take the following quotation from the
Mawāqif of Niffarī, an author with whom
we shall become better acquainted as we
proceed :

   " God said to me, ' The least of the
sciences of nearness is that you should
see in everything the effects of beholding Me, and that this vision should pre-
vail over you more than your gnosis of
Me.' "
Explanation by the commentator :
   " He means that the least of the
sciences of nearness (proximity to God)
is that when you look at anything,
sensibly or intellectually or otherwise,
you should be conscious of beholding
God with a vision clearer than your
vision of that thing.   There are diverse

degrees in this matter. Some mystics say that they never see anything without seeing God before it. Others say, ' without seeing God after it,' or ' with it '; or they say that they see nothing but God. A certain Sūfī said, ' I made the pilgrimage and saw the Ka'ba, but not the Lord of the Ka'ba.' This is the perception of one who is veiled. Then he said, ' I made the pilgrimage again, and I saw both the Ka'ba and the Lord of the Ka'ba.' This is contemplation of the Self - subsistence through which everything subsists, *i.e.* he saw the Ka'ba subsisting through the Lord of the Ka'ba. Then he said, ' I made the pilgrimage a third time, and I saw the Lord of the Ka'ba, but not the Ka'ba.' This is the ' station ' of *waqfat* (passing-away in the essence). In the present case the author is referring to contemplation of the Self-subsistence."

So much concerning the theory of illumination. But, as Mephistopheles says, " *grau ist alle Theorie* "; and though to most of us the living experience is denied, we can hear its loudest echoes and feel its warmest afterglow in the poetry which it has created. Let me translate part of a Persian ode by the dervish-poet, Bābā Kūhī of Shīrāz, who died in 1050 A.D.

"In the market, in the cloister—only God I saw.
In the valley and on the mountain—only God I saw.
Him I have seen beside me oft in tribulation;
In favour and in fortune—only God I saw.
In prayer and fasting, in praise and contemplation,
In the religion of the Prophet—only God I saw.
Neither soul nor body, accident nor substance,
Qualities nor causes—only God I saw.
I oped mine eyes and by the light of His face around
     me
In all the eye discovered—only God I saw.
Like a candle I was melting in His fire:
Amidst the flames outflashing—only God I saw.
Myself with mine own eyes I saw most clearly,
But when I looked with God's eyes—only God I saw.
I passed away into nothingness, I vanished,
And lo, I was the All-living—only God I saw."

The whole of Sūfism rests on the belief that when the individual self is lost, the Universal Self is found, or, in religious language, that ecstasy affords the only means by which the soul can directly communicate and become united with God. Asceticism, purification, love, gnosis, saintship—all the leading ideas of Sūfism—are developed from this cardinal principle.

Among the metaphorical terms commonly employed by the Sūfīs as, more or less, equivalent to ' ecstasy ' are *fanā* (passing-away), *wajd* (feeling), *samā'* (hearing), *dhawq* (taste), *shirb* (drinking), *ghaybat* (absence from self), *jadhbat* (attraction), *sukr* (intoxication), and *hāl* (emotion). It would be tedious and not, I think, specially instructive to examine in detail the definitions of those terms and of many others akin to them which occur in Sūfī text-books. We are not brought appreciably nearer to understanding the nature of ecstasy when it is described as "a divine mystery which God communicates to true believers who behold Him with the eye of certainty," or as "a flame which moves in the ground of the soul and is produced by love-desire." The Mohammedan theory of ecstasy, however, can hardly be discussed without reference to two of the above-mentioned technical expressions, namely, *fanā* and *samā'*.

As I have remarked in the Introduction (pp. 17-19), the term *fanā* includes different stages, aspects, and meanings. These may be summarised as follows :

1. A moral transformation of the soul through the extinction of all its passions and desires.

2. A mental abstraction or passing-away of the mind from all objects of perception, thoughts, actions, and feelings through its concentration upon the thought of God. Here the thought of God signifies contemplation of the divine attributes.

3. The cessation of all conscious thought. The highest stage of *fanā* is reached when even the consciousness of having attained *fanā* disappears. This is what the Sūfīs call 'the passing-away of passing-away'

(*fanā al-fanā*). The mystic is now rapt in contemplation of the divine essence.

The final stage of *fanā*, the complete passing-away from self, forms the prelude to *baqā*, 'continuance' or 'abiding' in God, and will be treated with greater fullness in Chapter VI.

The first stage closely resembles the Buddhistic Nirvāṇa. It is a 'passing-away' of evil qualities and states of mind, which involves the simultaneous 'continuance' of good qualities and states of mind. This is necessarily an ecstatic process, inasmuch as all the attributes of 'self' are evil in relation to God. No one can make himself perfectly moral, *i.e.* perfectly 'selfless.' This must be done for him, through 'a flash of the divine beauty' in his heart.

While the first stage refers to the moral 'self,' the second refers to the percipient and intellectual 'self.' Using the classification generally adopted by Christian mystics, we may regard the former as the consummation of the Purgative Life, and the latter as the goal of the Illuminative Life. The third and last stage constitutes the highest level of the Contemplative Life.

Often, though not invariably, *fanā* is accompanied by loss of sensation. Sarī al-Saqatī, a famous Sūfī of the third century, expressed the opinion that if a man in this state were struck on the face with a sword, he would not feel the blow. Abu 'l-Khayr al-Aqta' had a gangrene in his foot. The physicians declared that his foot must be amputated, but he would not allow this to be done. His disciples said, "Cut it off while he is praying, for he is then unconscious." The physicians acted on their advice, and when Abu 'l-Khayr finished his prayers he found that the amputation had taken place. It is difficult to see how any one far advanced in *fanā* could be capable of keeping the religious law—a point on which the orthodox mystics lay great emphasis. Here the doctrine of saintship comes in. God takes care to preserve His elect from disobedience to His commands. We are told that Bāyazīd, Shiblī, and other saints were continually in a state of rapture until the hour of prayer arrived; then they returned to consciousness, and after performing their prayers became enraptured again.

In theory, the ecstatic trance is involuntary, although certain conditions are recognised as being specially favourable to its occurrence. "It comes to a man through vision of the majesty of God and through revelation of the divine omnipotence to his heart." Such, for instance, was the case of Abū Hamza, who, while walking in the streets of Baghdād and meditating on the nearness of God, suddenly fell into an ecstasy and went on his way, neither seeing nor hearing, until he recovered his senses and found himself in

the desert.   Trances of this kind sometimes
lasted many weeks.   It is recorded of Sahl
ibn 'Abdallah that he used to remain in
ecstasy twenty-five days at a time, eating
no food ; yet he would answer questions put
to him by the doctors of theology, and even
in winter his shirt would be damp with sweat.
But the Sūfīs soon discovered that ecstasy
might be induced artificially, not only by
concentration of thought, recollection (*dhikr*),
and other innocent methods of autohypnosis,
but also by music, singing, and dancing.
These are included in the term *samā'*, which
properly means nothing more than audition.
   That Moslems are extraordinarily sus-
ceptible to the sweet influences of sound will
not be doubted by any one who remembers
how, in the *Arabian Nights*, heroes and
heroines alike swoon upon the slightest pro-
vocation afforded by a singing-girl touching
her lute and trilling a few lines of passionate
verse.   The fiction is true to life.   When
Sūfī writers discuss the analogous phenomena of ecstasy, they commonly do so in a
chapter entitled ' Concerning the *Samā'*.'
Under this heading Hujwīrī, in the final
chapter of his *Kashf al-Mahjūb*, gives us
an excellent summary of his own and
other Mohammedan theories, together with
numerous anecdotes of persons who were
thrown into ecstasy on hearing a verse of the
Koran or a heavenly voice (*hātif*) or poetry

or music. Many are said to have died from the emotion thus aroused. I may add by way of explanation that, according to a well-known mystical belief, God has inspired every created thing to praise Him in its own language, so that all the sounds in the universe form, as it were, one vast choral hymn by which He glorifies Himself. Consequently those whose hearts He has opened and endowed with spiritual perception hear His voice everywhere, and ecstasy overcomes them as they listen to the rhythmic chant of the muezzin, or the street cry of the saqqā shouldering his waterskin, or, perchance, to the noise of wind or the bleating of a sheep or the piping of a bird.

Pythagoras and Plato are responsible for another theory, to which the Sūfī poets frequently allude, that music awakens in the soul a memory of celestial harmonies heard in a state of pre-existence, before the soul was separated from God. Thus Jalāluddīn Rūmī :

"The song of the spheres in their revolutions
   Is what men sing with lute and voice.
   As we all are members of Adam,
   We have heard these melodies in Paradise.
   Though earth and water have cast their veil upon us,
   We retain faint reminiscences of these heavenly songs ;
   But while we are thus shrouded by gross earthly veils,
   How can the tones of the dancing spheres reach us ? " [1]

---

[1] E. H. Whinfield, abridged translation of the *Masnavī*, p. 182.

The formal practice of *samā'* quickly spread amongst the Sūfīs and produced an acute cleavage of opinion, some holding it to be lawful and praiseworthy, whilst others condemned it as an abominable innovation and incitement to vice. Hujwīrī adopts the middle view expressed in a saying of Dhu 'l-Nūn the Egyptian :

> " Music is a divine influence which stirs the heart to seek God : those who listen to it spiritually attain unto God, and those who listen to it sensually fall into unbelief."

He declares, in effect, that audition is neither good nor bad, and must be judged by its results.

> " When an anchorite goes into a tavern, the tavern becomes his cell, but when a wine-bibber goes into a cell, that cell becomes his tavern."

One whose heart is absorbed in the thought of God cannot be corrupted by hearing musical instruments. So with dancing.

> " When the heart throbs and rapture grows intense, and the agitation of ecstasy is manifested and conventional forms are gone, this is not dancing nor bodily indulgence, but a dissolution of the soul."

Hujwīrī, however, lays down several precautionary rules for those who engage in audition, and he confesses that the public concerts given by dervishes are extremely demoralising. Novices, he thinks, should not be permitted to attend them. In modern times these orgiastic scenes have frequently been described by eye-witnesses. I will now translate from Jāmī's *Lives of the Saints* the account of a similar performance which took place about seven hundred years ago.

"There was a certain dervish, a negro called Zangī Bashgirdī, who had attained to such a high degree of spirituality that the mystic dance could not be started until he came out and joined in it. One day, in the course of the *samā'*, he was seized with ecstasy, and rising into the air seated himself on a lofty arch which overlooked the dancers. In descending he leaped on to Majduddīn of Baghdād, and encircled with his legs the neck of the Sheykh, who nevertheless continued to spin round in the dance, though he was a very frail and slender man, whereas the negro was tall and heavy. When the dance was finished, Majduddīn said, 'I did not know whether it was a negro or a sparrow on my neck.' On getting off the Sheykh's shoulders, the negro bit his cheek so severely that the scar remained visible ever after. Majduddīn often used to say that on the Day of Judgment he would not boast of anything except that he bore the mark of this negro's teeth on his face."

Grotesque and ignoble features—not to speak of grosser deformities—must appear in any faithful delineation of the ecstatic life of Islam. Nothing is gained by concealing their existence or by minimising their importance. If, as Jalāluddīn Rūmī says :

" Men incur the reproach of wine and drugs
   That they may escape for a while from self-consciousness,
   Since all know this life to be a snare,
   Volitional memory and thought to be a hell,"

let us acknowledge that the transports of spiritual intoxication are not always sublime, and that human nature has a trick of avenging itself on those who would cast it off.

CHAPTER III

THE Sūfīs distinguish three organs of spiritual communication: the heart (*qalb*), which knows God; the spirit (*rūh*), which loves Him; and the inmost ground of the soul (*sirr*), which contemplates Him. It would take us into deep waters if we were to embark upon a discussion of these terms and their relation to each other. A few words concerning the first of the three will suffice. The *qalb*, though connected in some mysterious way with the physical heart, is not a thing of flesh and blood. Unlike the English 'heart,' its nature is rather intellectual than emotional, but whereas the intellect cannot gain real knowledge of God, the *qalb* is capable of knowing the essences of all things, and when illumined by faith and knowledge reflects the whole content of the divine mind; hence the Prophet said, "My earth and My heaven contain Me not, but the heart of My faithful servant containeth Me." This revelation, however, is a comparatively rare experience.

Normally, the heart is 'veiled,' blackened by sin, tarnished by sensual impressions and images, pulled to and fro between reason and passion : a battlefield on which the armies of God and the Devil contend for victory. Through one gate, the heart receives immediate knowledge of God ; through another, it lets in the illusions of sense. " Here a world and there a world," says Jalāluddīn Rūmī. " I am seated on the threshold." Therefore man is potentially lower than the brutes and higher than the angels.

> "Angel and brute man's wondrous leaven compose ;
> To these inclining, less than these he grows,
> But if he means the angel, more than those."

Less than the brutes, because they lack the knowledge that would enable them to rise ; more than the angels, because they are not subject to passion and so cannot fall.

How shall a man know God ? Not by the senses, for He is immaterial ; nor by the intellect, for He is unthinkable. Logic never gets beyond the finite ; philosophy sees double ; book - learning fosters self-conceit and obscures the idea of the Truth with clouds of empty words. Jalāluddīn Rūmī, addressing the scholastic theologian, asks scornfully :

> "Do you know a name without a thing answering to it ?
> Have you ever plucked a rose from R, O, S, E ?
> You name His name ; go, seek the reality named by it !

Look for the moon in the sky, not in the water!
If you desire to rise above mere names and letters,
Make yourself free from self at one stroke.
Become pure from all attributes of self,
That you may see your own bright essence,
Yea, see in your own heart the knowledge of the
    Prophet,
Without book, without tutor, without preceptor."

This knowledge comes by illumination, revelation, inspiration.

"Look in your own heart," says the Sūfī, "for the kingdom of God is within you." He who truly knows himself knows God, for the heart is a mirror in which every divine quality is reflected. But just as a steel mirror when coated with rust loses its power of reflexion, so the inward spiritual sense, which Sūfīs call the eye of the heart, is blind to the celestial glory until the dark obstruction of the phenomenal self, with all its sensual contaminations, has been wholly cleared away. The clearance, if it is to be done effectively, must be the work of God, though it demands a certain inward co-operation on the part of man. "Whosoever shall strive for Our sake, We will guide him into Our ways" (Kor. 29. 69). Action is false and vain, if it is thought to proceed from one's self, but the enlightened mystic regards God as the real agent in every act, and therefore takes no credit for his good works nor desires to be recompensed for them.

While ordinary knowledge is denoted by
the term *'ilm*, the mystic knowledge peculiar
to the Sūfīs is called *ma'rifat* or *'irfān*. As
I have indicated in the foregoing paragraphs,
ma'rifat is fundamentally different from *'ilm*,
and a different word must be used to
translate it. We need not look far for a
suitable equivalent. The *ma'rifat* of the
Sūfīs is the ' gnosis ' of Hellenistic theosophy,
i.e. direct knowledge of God based on
revelation or apocalyptic vision. It is not
the result of any mental process, but depends
entirely on the will and favour of God, who
bestows it as a gift from Himself upon
those whom He has created with the capacity
for receiving it. It is a light of divine
grace that flashes into the heart and
overwhelms every human faculty in its
dazzling beams. " He who knows [God is
dumb."

The relation of gnosis to positive religion
is discussed in a very remarkable treatise
on speculative mysticism by Niffarī, an
unknown wandering dervish who died in
Egypt in the latter half of the tenth century.
His work, consisting of a series of revelations
in which God addresses the writer and
instructs him concerning the theory of
gnosis, is couched in abstruse language and
would scarcely be intelligible without the
commentary which accompanies it ; but its
value as an original exposition of advanced

Sūfism will sufficiently appear from the excerpts given in this chapter.[1]

Those who seek God, says Niffarī, are of three kinds : *firstly*, the worshippers to whom God makes Himself known by means of bounty, *i.e.* they worship Him in the hope of winning Paradise or some spiritual recompense such as dreams and miracles ; *secondly*, the philosophers and scholastic theologians, to whom God makes Himself known by means of glory, *i.e.* they can never find the glorious God whom they seek, wherefore they assert that His essence is unknowable, saying, " We know that we know Him not, and that is our knowledge " ; *thirdly*, the gnostics, to whom God makes Himself known by means of ecstasy, *i.e.* they are possessed and controlled by a rapture that deprives them of the consciousness of individual existence.

Niffarī bids the gnostic perform only such acts of worship as are in accordance with his vision of God, though in so doing he will necessarily disobey the religious law which was made for the vulgar. His inward feeling must decide how far the external forms of religion are good for him.

" God said to me, Ask Me and say, ' O Lord, how shall I cleave to Thee, so that when my day (of judgment)

[1] I am now engaged in preparing an edition of the Arabic text, together with an English translation and commentary.

comes, Thou wilt not punish me nor avert Thy face from me ? ' Then I will answer thee and say, ' Cleave in thy outward theory and practice to the Sunna (the rule of the Prophet), and cleave in thy inward feeling to the gnosis which I have given thee ; and know that when I make Myself known to thee, I will not accept from thee anything of the Sunna but what My gnosis brings to thee, because thou art one of those to whom I speak : thou hearest Me and knowest that thou hearest Me, and thou seest that I am the source of all things.' "

The commentator observes that the Sunna, being general in scope, makes no distinction between individuals, *e.g.* seekers of Paradise and seekers of God, but that in reality it contains exactly what each person requires. The portion specially appropriate in every case is discerned either by means of gnosis, which God communicates to the heart, or by means of guidance imparted by a spiritual director.

" And He said to me, ' My exoteric revelation does not support My esoteric revelation.' "

This means that the gnostic need not be dismayed if his inner experience conflicts with the religious law. The contradiction is only apparent. Religion addresses itself

to the common herd of men who are veiled
by their minds, by logic, tradition, and so
on; whereas gnosis belongs to the elect,
whose bodies and spirits are bathed in the
eternal Light. Religion sees things from
the aspect of plurality, but gnosis regards
the all-embracing Unity. Hence the same
act is good in religion, but evil in gnosis—
a truth which is briefly stated thus :

> " The good deeds of the pious are the
> ill deeds of the favourites of God."

Although works of devotion are not incompatible with gnosis, no one who connects
them in the slightest degree with himself
is a gnostic. This is the theme of the following allegory. Niffarī seldom writes so
lucidly as he does here, yet I fancy that
few of my readers will find the explanations
printed within square brackets altogether
superfluous.

The Revelation of the Sea

> " God bade me behold the Sea, and I
> saw the ships sinking and the planks
> floating ; then the planks too were
> submerged."

[The Sea denotes the spiritual experiences through which the mystic
passes in his journey to God. The
point at issue is this : whether he
should prefer the religious law or dis-

interested love. Here he is warned not to rely on his good works, which are no better than sinking ships and will never bring him safely to port. No ; if he would attain to God, he must rely on God alone. If he does not rely entirely on God, but lets himself trust ever so little in anything else, he is still clinging to a plank. Though his trust in God is greater than before, it is not yet complete.]

"And He said to me, 'Those who voyage are not saved.'"

[The voyager uses the ship as a means of crossing the sea : therefore he relies, not on the First Cause, but on secondary causes.]

"And He said to me, 'Those who instead of voyaging cast themselves into the Sea take a risk.'"

[To abandon all secondary causes is like plunging in the sea. The mystic who makes this venture is in jeopardy, for two reasons : he may regard himself, not God, as initiating and carrying out the action of abandonment,—and one who renounces a thing through 'self' is in worse case than if he had not renounced it,—or he may abandon secondary causes (good works, hope of Paradise, etc.), not for God's sake, but from sheer indifference and lack of spiritual feeling.]

" And He said to me, ' Those who voyage and take no risk shall perish.' "

[Notwithstanding the dangers referred to, he must make God his sole object or fail.]

" And He said to me, ' In taking the risk there is a part of salvation.' "

[Only a part of salvation, because perfect selflessness has not yet been attained. The whole of salvation consists in the effacement of all secondary causes, all phenomena, through the rapture which results from vision of God. But this is gnosis, and the present revelation is addressed to mystics of a lower grade. The gnostic takes no risk, for he has nothing to lose.]

" And the wave came and lifted those beneath it and overran the shore."

[Those beneath the wave are they who voyage in ships and consequently suffer shipwreck. Their reliance on secondary causes casts them ashore, *i.e.* brings them back to the world of phenomena whereby they are veiled from God.]

" And He said to me, ' The surface of the Sea is a gleam that cannot be reached.' "

[Any one who depends on external rites of worship to lead him to God is following a will-o'-the-wisp.]

" And its bottom is a darkness impenetrable."

[To discard positive religion, root and branch, is to wander in a pathless maze.]

" And between the two are fishes which are to be feared."

[He refers to the middle way between pure exotericism and pure esotericism. The ' fishes ' are its perils and obstacles.]

" Do not voyage on the Sea, lest I cause thee to be veiled by the vehicle."

[The ' vehicle ' signifies the ' ship,' *i.e.* reliance on something other than God.]

" And do not cast thyself into the Sea, lest I cause thee to be veiled by thy casting thyself."

[Whoever regards any act as his own act and attributes it to himself is far from God.]

" And He said to me, ' In the Sea are boundaries : which of them will bear thee on ? ' "

[The ' boundaries ' are the various degrees of spiritual experience. The mystic ought not to rely on any of these, for they are all imperfect.]

" And He said to me, ' If thou givest thyself to the Sea and sinkest therein, thou wilt fall a prey to one of its beasts.' "

[If the mystic either relies on secondary causes or abandons them by his own act, he will go astray.]

" And He said to me, ' I deceive thee if I direct thee to aught save Myself.' "

[If the mystic's inward voice bids him turn to anything except God, it deceives him.]

" And He said to me, ' If thou perishest for the sake of other than Me, thou wilt belong to that for which thou hast perished.'

" And He said to me, ' This world belongs to him whom I have turned away from it and from whom I have turned it away; and the next world belongs to him towards whom have brought it and whom I have brought towards Myself.' "

[He means to say that everlasting joy is the portion of those whose hearts are turned away from this world and who have no worldly possessions. They really enjoy this world, because it cannot separate them from God. Similarly, the true owners of the next world are those who do not seek it, inasmuch as it is not the real object of their desire, but contemplate God alone.]

The gnostic descries the element of reality in positive religion, but his gnosis is not derived from religion or from any sort of human knowledge : it is properly concerned with the divine attributes, and God Himself reveals the knowledge of these to His saints who contemplate Him. Dhu 'l-Nūn of Egypt, whose mystical speculations mark him out as the father of Moslem theosophy, said that gnostics are not themselves, and do not subsist through themselves, but so far as they subsist, they subsist through God.

> " They move as God causes them to move, and their words are the words of God which roll upon their tongues, and their sight is the sight of God which has entered their eyes."

The gnostic contemplates the attributes of God, not His essence, for even in gnosis a small trace of duality remains : this disappears only in *fanā al-fanā*, the total passing-away in the undifferentiated Godhead. The cardinal attribute of God is unity, and the divine unity is the first and last principle of gnosis.[1]

Both Moslem and Sūfī declare that God is One, but the statement bears a different meaning in each instance. The Moslem means that God is unique in His essence, qualities, and acts; that He is absolutely unlike all other beings. The Sūfī means

[1] According to some mystics, the gnosis of unity constitutes a higher stage which is called 'the Truth' (*haqīqat*). See above, p. 29.

that God is the One Real Being which
underlies all phenomena. This principle is
carried to its extreme consequences, as we
shall see. If nothing except God exists,
then the whole universe, including man, is
essentially one with God, whether it is
regarded as an emanation which proceeds
from Him, without impairing His unity,
like sunbeams from the sun, or whether it is
conceived as a mirror in which the divine
attributes are reflected. But surely a God
who is all in all can have no reason for
thus revealing Himself : why should the One
pass over into the Many ? The Sūfīs answer
—a philosopher would say that they evade
the difficulty—by quoting the famous Tradition : " I was a hidden treasure and I desired
to be known ; therefore I created the creation in order that I might be known." In
other words, God is the eternal Beauty,
and it lies in the nature of beauty to desire
love. The mystic poets have described the
self-manifestation of the One with a pro-
fusion of splendid imagery. Jāmī says, for
example :

" From all eternity the Beloved unveiled His beauty in
        the solitude of the unseen ;
    He held up the mirror to His own face, He displayed
        His loveliness to Himself.
    He was both the spectator and the spectacle ; no eye
        but His had surveyed the Universe.
    All was One, there was no duality, no pretence of
        ' mine ' or ' thine.'

The vast orb of Heaven, with its myriad incomings and
    outgoings, was concealed in a single point.
The Creation lay cradled in the sleep of non-existence,
    like a child ere it has breathed.
The eye of the Beloved, seeing what was not, regarded
    nonentity as existent.
Although He beheld His attributes and qualities as a
    perfect whole in His own essence,
Yet He desired that they should be displayed to Him
    in another mirror,
And that each one of His eternal attributes should be-
    come manifest accordingly in a diverse form.
Therefore He created the verdant fields of Time and
    Space and the life-giving garden of the world,
That every branch and leaf and fruit might show forth
    His various perfections.
The cypress gave a hint of His comely stature, the rose
    gave tidings of His beauteous countenance.
Wherever Beauty peeped out, Love appeared beside it ;
    wherever Beauty shone in a rosy cheek, Love lit
    his torch from that flame.
Wherever Beauty dwelt in dark tresses, Love came and
    found a heart entangled in their coils.
Beauty and Love are as body and soul ; Beauty is the
    mine and Love the precious stone.
They have always been together from the very first ;
    never have they travelled but in each other's
    company."

In another work Jāmī sets forth the
relation of God to the world more philo-
sophically, as follows :
    " The unique Substance, viewed as
absolute and void of all phenomena, all
limitations and all multiplicity, is the
Real (*al-Haqq*). On the other hand,
viewed in His aspect of multiplicity and

plurality, under which He displays Himself when clothed with phenomena, He is the whole created universe. Therefore the universe is the outward visible expression of the Real, and the Real is the inner unseen reality of the universe. The universe before it was evolved to outward view was identical with the Real ; and the Real after this evolution is identical with the universe."

Phenomena, as such, are not-being and only derive a contingent existence from the qualities of Absolute Being by which they are irradiated. The sensible world resembles the fiery circle made by a single spark whirling round rapidly.

Man is the crown and final cause of the universe. Though last in the order of creation he is first in the process of divine thought, for the essential part of him is the primal Intelligence or universal Reason which emanates immediately from the Godhead. This corresponds to the Logos— the animating principle of all things—and is identified with the Prophet Mohammed. An interesting parallel might be drawn here between the Christian and Sūfī doctrines. The same expressions are applied to the founder of Islam which are used by St. John, St. Paul, and later mystical theologians concerning Christ. Thus, Mohammed is called the Light of God, he is said to have

existed before the creation of the world,
he is adored as the source of all life, actual
and possible, he is the Perfect Man in whom
all the divine attributes are manifested,
and a Sūfī tradition ascribes to him the
saying, " He that hath seen me hath seen
Allah." In the Moslem scheme, however,
the Logos doctrine occupies a subordinate
place, as it obviously must when the whole
duty of man is believed to consist in realising
the unity of God. The most distinctive
feature of Oriental as opposed to European
mysticism is its profound consciousness of
an omnipresent, all-pervading unity in which
every vestige of individuality is swallowed
up. Not to become *like* God or *personally*
to participate in the divine nature is the
Sūfī's aim, but to escape from the bondage
of his unreal selfhood and thereby to be
reunited with the One infinite Being.

According to Jāmī, Unification consists
in making the heart single—that is, in purify-
ing and divesting it of attachment to aught
except God, both in respect of desire and
will and also as regards knowledge and
gnosis. The mystic's desire and will should
be severed from all things which are desired
and willed ; all objects of knowledge and
understanding should be removed from his
intellectual vision. His thoughts should be
directed solely towards God, he should not
be conscious of anything besides.

So long as he is a captive in the snare of
passion and lust, it is hard for him to main-
tain this relation to God, but when the subtle
influence of that attraction becomes manifest
in him, expelling preoccupation with objects
of sense and cognition from his inward
being, delight in that divine communion
prevails over bodily pleasures and spiritual
joys ; the painful task of self-mortification
is ended, and the sweetness of contemplation
enravishes his soul.

When the sincere aspirant perceives in
himself the beginning of this attraction,
which is delight in the recollection of God,
let him fix his whole mind on fostering
and strengthening it, let him keep himself
aloof from whatsoever is incompatible with
it, and deem that even though he were to
devote an eternity to cultivating that communion, he would have done nothing and
would not have discharged his duty as he
ought.

> " Love thrilled the chord of love in my soul's lute,
> And changed me all to love from head to foot.
> 'Twas but a moment's touch, yet shall Time ever
> To me the debt of thanksgiving impute."

It is an axiom of the Sūfīs that what is
not *in* a man he cannot know. The gnostic
—Man *par excellence*—could not know God
and all the mysteries of the universe, unless
he found them in himself. He is the micro-

cosm, ' a copy made in the image of God,'
' the eye of the world whereby God sees
His own works.' In knowing himself as he
really is, he knows God, and he knows himself through God, who is nearer to everything
than its knowledge of itself. Knowledge
of God precedes, and is the cause of, self-
knowledge.

Gnosis, then, is unification, realisation of
the fact that the appearance of ' otherness '
beside Oneness is a false and deluding
dream. Gnosis lays this spectre, which
haunts unenlightened men all their lives ;
which rises, like a wall of utter darkness,
between them and God. Gnosis proclaims
that ' I ' is a figure of speech, and that one
cannot truly refer any will, feeling, thought,
or action to one's self.

Niffarī heard the divine voice saying to
him :

> " When thou regardest thyself as
> existent and dost not regard Me as the
> Cause of thy existence, I veil My face
> and thine own face appears to thee.
> Therefore consider what is displayed
> to thee, and what is hidden from
> thee ! "

[If a man regards himself as existing
through God, that which is of God in
him predominates over the phenomenal
element and makes it pass away, so that
he sees nothing but God. If, on the

contrary, he regards himself as having an independent existence, his unreal egoism is displayed to him and the reality of God becomes hidden from him.]

" Regard neither My displaying nor that which is displayed, else thou wilt laugh and weep ; and when thou laughest and weepest, thou art thine, not Mine."

[He who regards the act of divine revelation is guilty of polytheism, since revelation involves both a revealing subject and a revealed object ; and he who regards the revealed object which is part of the created universe, regards something other than God. Laughter signifies joy for what you have gained, and weeping denotes grief for what you have lost. Both are selfish actions. The gnostic neither laughs nor weeps.]

" If thou dost not put behind thee all that I have displayed and am displaying, thou wilt not prosper ; and unless thou prosper, thou wilt not become concentrated upon Me."

[Prosperity is true belief in God, which requires complete abstraction from created things.]

Logically, these doctrines annul every moral and religious law. In the gnostic's vision there are no divine rewards and punishments, no human standards of right

and wrong. For him, the written word
of God has been abrogated by a direct
and intimate revelation.

"I do not say," exclaimed Abu
'l-Hasan Khurqānī, "that Paradise and
Hell are non-existent, but I say that they
are nothing to me, because God created
them both, and there is no room for any
created object in the place where I
am."

From this standpoint all types of religion
are equal, and Islam is no better than
idolatry. It does not matter what creed a
man professes or what rites he performs.

"The true mosque in a pure and holy heart
Is builded: there let all men worship God;
For there He dwells, not in a mosque of stone."

Amidst all the variety of creeds and worshippers the gnostic sees but one real object
of worship.

"Those who adore God in the sun"
(says Ibn al-'Arabī) "behold the sun,
and those who adore Him in living
things see a living thing, and those who
adore Him in lifeless things see a lifeless thing, and those who adore Him
as a Being unique and unparalleled
see that which has no like. Do not
attach yourself" (he continues) "to any
particular creed exclusively, so that you
disbelieve in all the rest; otherwise,

you will lose much good, nay, you will
fail to recognise the real truth of the
matter. God, the omnipresent and
omnipotent, is not limited by any one
creed, for He says (Kor. 2. 109),
' Wheresoever ye turn, there is the face
of Allah.' Every one praises what he
believes ; his god is his own creature,
and in praising it he praises himself.
Consequently he blames the beliefs of
others, which he would not do if he were
just, but his dislike is based on ignorance. If he knew Junayd's saying,
' The water takes its colour from the
vessel containing it,' he would not interfere with other men's beliefs, but
would perceive God in every form of
belief."

And Hafiz sings, more in the spirit of the
freethinker, perhaps, than of the mystic :

> " Love is where the glory falls
> Of Thy face—on convent walls
> Or on tavern floors, the same
> Unextinguishable flame.
>
> Where the turbaned anchorite
> Chanteth Allah day and night,
> Church bells ring the call to prayer
> And the Cross of Christ is there."

Sūfism may join hands with freethought—
it has often done so—but hardly ever with
sectarianism. This explains why the vast

majority of Sūfīs have been, at least nomin-
ally, attached to the catholic body of the
Moslem community. 'Abdallah Ansārī declared that of two thousand Sūfī Sheykhs
with whom he was acquainted only two were
Shī'ites. A certain man who was a descend-
ant of the Caliph 'Alī, and a fanatical
Shī'ite, tells the following story :

" For five years," he said, " my father
sent me daily to a spiritual director.
I learned one useful lesson from him :
he told me that I should never know
anything at all about Sūfism until I
got completely rid of the pride which
I felt on account of my lineage."

Superficial observers have described
Bābism as an offshoot of Sūfism, but the
dogmatism of the one is naturally opposed
to the broad eclecticism of the other. In
proportion as the Sūfī gains more knowledge
of God, his religious prejudices are diminished.
Sheykh 'Abd al-Rahīm ibn al-Sabbāgh, who
at first disliked living in Upper Egypt, with
its large Jewish and Christian population,
said in his old age that he would as readily em-
brace a Jew or Christian as one of his own faith.

While the innumerable forms of creed and
ritual may be regarded as having a certain
relative value in so far as the inward feeling
which inspires them is ever one and the same,
from another aspect they seem to be veils
of the Truth, barriers which the zealous

Unitarian must strive to abolish and destroy.

> "This world and that world are the egg, and the bird within it
>   Is in darkness and broken-winged and scorned and despised.
>   Regard unbelief and faith as the white and the yolk in this egg,
>   Between them, joining and dividing, a barrier which they shall not pass.
>   When He hath graciously fostered the egg under His wing,
>   Infidelity and religion disappear: the bird of Unity spreads its pinions."

The great Persian mystic, Abū Saʻīd ibn Abi 'l-Khayr, speaking in the name of the Calendars or wandering dervishes, expresses their iconoclastic principles with astonishing boldness:

> "Not until every mosque beneath the sun
>   Lies ruined, will our holy work be done;
>   And never will true Musalmān appear
>   Till faith and infidelity are one."

Such open declarations of war against the Mohammedan religion are exceptional. Notwithstanding the breadth and depth of the gulf between full-blown Sūfism and orthodox Islam, many, if not most, Sūfīs have paid homage to the Prophet and have observed the outward forms of devotion which are incumbent on all Moslems. They have invested these rites and ceremonies with a new meaning; they have allegorised them,

but they have not abandoned them. Take
the pilgrimage, for example. In the eyes
of the genuine Sūfī it is null and void
unless each of the successive religious acts
which it involves is accompanied by corresponding ' movements of the heart.'

A man who had just returned from the
pilgrimage came to Junayd. Junayd said :
"From the hour when you first journeyed from your home have you also
been journeying away from all sins ? "
He said " No."   " Then," said Junayd,
" you have made no journey. At every
stage where you halted for the night
did you traverse a station on the way
to God ? "   " No," he replied. " Then,"
said Junayd, " you have not trodden
the road, stage by stage. When you put
on the pilgrim's garb at the proper place,
did you discard the qualities of human
nature as you cast off your clothes ? "
" No."   " Then you have not put on
the pilgrim's garb. When you stood at
'Arafāt, did you stand one moment in
contemplation of God ? "   " No." " Then
you have not stood at 'Arafāt. When
you went to Muzdalifa and achieved your
desire, did you renounce all sensual
desires ? "   " No."   " Then you have
not gone to Muzdalifa. When you
circumambulated the Ka'ba, did you
behold the immaterial beauty of God

in the abode of purification ? "   " No."
" Then you have not circumambulated
the Ka'ba.   When you ran between
Safā and Marwa, did you attain to
purity (safā) and virtue (muruwwat) ? "
" No."   " Then you have not run.
When you came to Minā, did all your
wishes (munā) cease ? "   " No."   " Then
you have not yet visited Minā.   When
you reached the slaughter-place and
offered sacrifice, did you sacrifice the
objects of worldly desire ? "   " No."
" Then you have not sacrificed.   When
you threw the pebbles, did you throw
away whatever sensual thoughts were
accompanying you ? "   " No."   " Then
you have not yet thrown the pebbles,
and you have not yet performed the
pilgrimage."
This anecdote contrasts the outer religious
law of theology with the inner spiritual truth
of mysticism, and shows that they should
not be divorced from each other.
     " The Law without the Truth," says
Hujwīrī, " is ostentation, and the Truth
without the Law is hypocrisy.   Their
mutual relation may be compared to
that of body and spirit : when the spirit
departs from the body, the living body
becomes   a   corpse,   and   the   spirit
vanishes like wind.   The Moslem profession of faith includes both :   the

words, 'There is no god but Allah,' are the Truth, and the words, ' Mohammed is the apostle of Allah,' are the Law ; any one who denies the Truth is an infidel, and any one who rejects the Law is a heretic."

Middle ways, though proverbially safe, are difficult to walk in ; and only by a *tour de force* can the Koran be brought into line with the esoteric doctrine which the Sūfīs derive from it. Undoubtedly they have done a great work for Islam. They have deepened and enriched the lives of millions by ruthlessly stripping off the husk of religion and insisting that its kernel must be sought, not in any formal act, but in cultivation of spiritual feelings and in purification of the inward man. This was a legitimate and most fruitful development of the Prophet's teaching. But the Prophet was a strict monotheist, while the Sūfīs, whatever they may pretend or imagine, are theosophists, pantheists, or monists. When they speak and write as believers in the dogmas of positive religion, they use language which cannot be reconciled with such a theory of unity as we are now examining. 'Afīfuddīn al-Tilimsānī, from whose commentary on Niffarī I have given some extracts in this chapter, said roundly that the whole Koran is polytheism—a perfectly just statement from the monistic point of view, though few Sūfīs have dared to be so explicit.

The mystic Unitarians admit the appearance of contradiction, but deny its reality. "The Law and the Truth" (they might say) "are the same thing in different aspects. The Law is for you, the Truth for us. In addressing you we speak according to the measure of your understanding, since what is meat for gnostics is poison to the uninitiated, and the highest mysteries ought to be jealously guarded from profane ears. It is only human reason that sees the single as double, and balances the Law against the Truth. Pass away from the world of opposites and become one with God, who has no opposite."

The gnostic recognises that the Law is valid and necessary in the moral sphere. While good and evil remain, the Law stands over both, commanding and forbidding, rewarding and punishing. He knows, on the other hand, that only God really exists and acts: therefore, if evil really exists, it must be divine, and if evil things are really done, God must be the doer of them. The conclusion is false because the hypothesis is false. Evil has no real existence; it is not-being, which is the privation and absence of being, just as darkness is the absence of light. "Once," said Nūrī, "I beheld the Light, and I fixed my gaze upon it until I became the Light." No wonder that such illuminated souls, supremely indifferent to the shadow-shows of religion and morality in a phantom world, are ready to cry with Jalāluddīn :

"The man of God is made wise by the Truth,
The man of God is not learned from book.
The man of God is beyond infidelity and faith,
To the man of God right and wrong are alike."

It must be borne in mind that this is a theory of perfection, and that those whom it exalts above the Law are saints, spiritual guides, and profound theosophists who enjoy the special favour of God and presumably do not need to be restrained, coerced, or punished. In practice, of course, it leads in many instances to antinomianism and libertinism, as among the Bektāshīs and other orders of the so-called ' lawless ' dervishes. The same theories produced the same results in Europe during the Middle Ages, and the impartial historian cannot ignore the corruptions to which a purely subjective mysticism is liable ; but on the present occasion we are concerned with the rose itself, not with its cankers.

Not all Sūfīs are gnostics ; and, as I have mentioned before, those who are not yet ripe for the gnosis receive from their gnostic teachers the ethical instruction suitable to their needs. Jalāluddīn Rūmī, in his collection of lyrical poems entitled *The Dīvān*

of Shamsi Tabrīz, gives free rein to a pantheistic enthusiasm which sees all things
under the form of eternity.

"I have put duality away, I have seen that the two
    worlds are one;
  One I seek, One I know, One I see, One I call.
  I am intoxicated with Love's cup, the two worlds have
    passed out of my ken;
  I have no business save carouse and revelry."

But in his *Masnavī*—a work so famous and
venerated that it has been styled ' The Koran
of Persia '—we find him in a more sober
mood expounding the Sūfī doctrines and
justifying the ways of God to man. Here,
though he is a convinced optimist and agrees
with Ghazālī that this is the best of all
possible worlds, he does not airily dismiss the
problem of evil as something outside reality,
but endeavours to show that evil, or what
seems evil to us, is part of the divine order
and harmony. I will quote some passages of
his argument and leave my readers to judge
how far it is successful or, at any rate,
suggestive.

The Sūfīs, it will be remembered, conceive
the universe as a projected and reflected image
of God. The divine light, streaming forth
in a series of emanations, falls at last upon
the darkness of not-being, every atom of which
reflects some attribute of Deity. For instance,
the beautiful attributes of love and mercy
are reflected in the form of heaven and the

angels, while the terrible attributes of wrath
and vengeance are reflected in the form of
hell and the devils. Man reflects all the
attributes, the terrible as well as the
beautiful : he is an epitome of heaven and
hell. Omar Khayyām alludes to this theory
when he says :

> "Hell is a spark from our fruitless pain,
> Heaven a breath from our time of joy"

—a couplet which Fitz Gerald moulded into
the magnificent stanza :

> "Heav'n but the Vision of fulfilled Desire,
> And Hell the Shadow from a Soul on fire,
> Cast on the Darkness into which Ourselves
> So late emerged from, shall so soon expire."

Jalāluddīn, therefore, does in a sense make
God the author of evil, but at the same time
he makes evil intrinsically good in relation
to God—for it is the reflexion of certain
divine attributes which in themselves are
absolutely good. So far as evil is really evil,
it springs from not-being. The poet assigns
a different value to this term in its relation to
God and in its relation to man. In respect
of God not-being is nothing, for God is real
Being, but in man it is the principle of evil
which constitutes half of human nature. In
the one case it is a pure negation, in the
other it is positively and actively pernicious.
We need not quarrel with the poet for

coming to grief in his logic. There are some occasions when intense moral feeling is worth any amount of accurate thinking.

It is evident that the doctrine of divine unity implies predestination. Where God is and naught beside Him, there can be no other agent than He, no act but His. " Thou didst not throw, when thou threwest, but God threw " (Kor. 8. 17). Compulsion is felt only by those who do not love. To know God is to love Him ; and the gnostic may answer, like the dervish who was asked how he fared :

> "I fare as one by whose majestic will
> The world revolves, floods rise and rivers flow,
> Stars in their courses move ; yea, death and life
> Hang on his nod and fly to the ends of earth,
> His ministers of mourning or of joy."

This is the Truth ; but for the benefit of such as cannot bear it, Jalāluddīn vindicates the justice of God by asserting that men have the power to choose how they will act, although their freedom is subordinate to the divine will. Approaching the question, "Why does God ordain and create evil ? " he points out that things are known through their opposites, and that the existence of evil is necessary for the manifestation of good.

> "Not-being and defect, wherever seen,
> Are mirrors of the beauty of all that is.
> The bone-setter, where should he try his skill

But on the patient lying with broken leg?
Were no base copper in the crucible,
How could the alchemist his craft display?"

Moreover, the divine omnipotence would not be completely realised if evil had remained uncreated.

"He is the source of evil, as thou sayest,
Yet evil hurts Him not. To make that evil
Denotes in Him perfection. Hear from me
A parable. The heavenly Artist paints
Beautiful shapes and ugly: in one picture
The loveliest women in the land of Egypt
Gazing on youthful Joseph amorously;
And lo, another scene by the same hand,
Hell-fire and Iblīs with his hideous crew:
Both master-works, created for good ends,
To show His perfect wisdom and confound
The sceptics who deny His mastery.
Could He not evil make, He would lack skill;
Therefore He fashions infidel alike
And Moslem true, that both may witness bear
To Him, and worship One Almighty Lord."

In reply to the objection that a God who creates evil must Himself be evil, Jalāluddīn, pursuing the analogy drawn from Art, remarks that ugliness in the picture is no evidence of ugliness in the painter.

Again, without evil it would be impossible to win the proved virtue which is the reward of self-conquest. Bread must be broken before it can serve as food, and grapes will not yield wine till they are crushed. Many men are led through tribulation to happiness.

As evil ebbs, good flows. Finally, much evil is only apparent. What seems a curse to one may be a blessing to another; nay, evil itself is turned to good for the righteous. Jalāluddīn will not admit that anything is absolutely bad.

> " Fools buy false coins because they are like the true.
>   If in the world no genuine minted coin
>   Were current, how would forgers pass the false?
>   Falsehood were nothing unless truth were there,
>   To make it specious. 'Tis the love of right
>   Lures men to wrong. Let poison but be mixed
>   With sugar, they will cram it into their mouths.
>   Oh, cry not that all creeds are vain! Some scent
>   Of truth they have, else they would not beguile.
>   Say not, 'How utterly fantastical!'
>   No fancy in the world is all untrue.
>   Amongst the crowd of dervishes hides one,
>   One true fakīr. Search well and thou wilt find!"

Surely this is a noteworthy doctrine. Jalāluddīn died only a few years after the birth of Dante, but the Christian poet falls far below the level of charity and tolerance reached by his Moslem contemporary.

How is it possible to discern the soul of goodness in things evil? By means of love, says Jalāluddīn, and the knowledge which love alone can give, according to the word of God in the holy Tradition :

> " My servant draws nigh unto Me, and I love him; and when I love him, I am his ear, so that he hears by Me, and his eye, so that he sees by Me, and his

tongue, so that he speaks by Me, and his hand, so that he takes by Me."

Although it will be convenient to treat of mystical love in a separate chapter, the reader must not fancy that a new subject is opening before him. Gnosis and love are spiritually identical; they teach the same truths in different language.

CHAPTER IV

DIVINE LOVE

ANY one acquainted, however slightly, with the mystical poetry of Islam must have remarked that the aspiration of the soul towards God is expressed, as a rule, in almost the same terms which might be used by an Oriental Anacreon or Herrick. The resemblance, indeed, is often so close that, unless we have some clue to the poet's intention, we are left in doubt as to his meaning. In some cases, perhaps, the ambiguity serves an artistic purpose, as in the odes of Ḥāfiz, but even when the poet is not deliberately keeping his readers suspended between earth and heaven, it is quite easy to mistake a mystical hymn for a drinking-song or a serenade. Ibn al-ʿArabī, the greatest theosophist whom the Arabs have produced, found himself obliged to write a commentary on some of his poems in order to refute the scandalous charge that they were designed to celebrate the charms of his mistress. Here are a few lines :

" Oh, her beauty—the tender maid! Its brilliance gives
light like lamps to one travelling in the dark.

She is a pearl hidden in a shell of hair as black as
    jet,
A pearl for which Thought dives and remains un-
    ceasingly in the deeps of that ocean.
He who looks upon her deems her to be a gazelle of
    the sand-hills, because of her shapely neck and
    the loveliness of her gestures."

It has been said that the Sūfīs invented
this figurative style as a mask for mysteries
which they desired to keep secret. That
desire was natural in those who proudly
claimed to possess an esoteric doctrine
known only to themselves; moreover, a
plain statement of what they believed might
have endangered their liberties, if not their
lives. But, apart from any such motives, the
Sūfīs adopt the symbolic style because there
is no other possible way of interpreting
mystical experience. So little does knowledge of the infinite revealed in ecstatic vision
need an artificial disguise that it cannot be
communicated at all except through types
and emblems drawn from the sensible world,
which, imperfect as they are, may suggest
and shadow forth a deeper meaning than
appears on the surface. " Gnostics," says
Ibn al-'Arabī, " cannot impart their feelings
to other men; they can only indicate them
symbolically to those who have begun to
experience the like." What kind of symbolism each mystic will prefer depends on
his temperament and character. If he be a

religious artist, a spiritual poet, his ideas of
reality are likely to clothe themselves in-
stinctively in forms of beauty and glowing
images of human love. To him the rosy
cheek of the beloved represents the divine
essence manifested through its attributes ;
her dark curls signify the One veiled by the
Many ; when he says, " Drink wine that it
may set you free from yourself," he means,
" Lose your phenomenal self in the rapture
of divine contemplation."   I might fill pages
with further examples.

This erotic and bacchanalian symbolism
is not, of course, peculiar to the mystical
poetry of Islam, but nowhere else is it displayed so opulently and in such perfection.
It has often been misunderstood by European critics, one of whom even now can
describe the ecstasies of the Sūfīs as " inspired partly by wine and strongly tinged
with sensuality." As regards the whole
body of Sūfīs, the charge is altogether false.
No intelligent and unprejudiced student
of their writings could have made it, and
we ought to have been informed on what
sort of evidence it is based. There are black
sheep in every flock, and amongst the Sūfīs
we find many hypocrites, debauchees, and
drunkards who bring discredit on the pure
brethren. But it is just as unfair to judge
Sūfism in general by the excesses of these
impostors as it would be to condemn all

Christian mysticism on the ground that certain sects and individuals are immoral.

> "God is the Sāqī[1] and the Wine:
> He knows what manner of love is mine,"

said Jalāluddīn. Ibn al-ʿArabī declares that no religion is more sublime than a religion of love and longing for God. Love is the essence of all creeds: the true mystic welcomes it whatever guise it may assume.

> "My heart has become capable of every form: it is a pasture for gazelles and a convent for Christian monks,
> And a temple for idols, and the pilgrim's Kaʿba, and the tables of the Tora and the book of the Koran.
> I follow the religion of Love, whichever way his camels take. My religion and my faith is the true religion.
> We have a pattern in Bishr, the lover of Hind and her sister, and in Qays and Lubnā, and in Mayya and Ghaylān."

Commenting on the last verse, the poet writes :

> " Love, *quâ* love, is one and the same reality to those Arab lovers and to me; but the objects of our love are different, for they loved a phenomenon, whereas I love the Real. They are a pattern to us, because God only afflicted them with love for human beings in order that He might show, by means of them, the

[1] Cupbearer.

falseness of those who pretend to love
Him, and yet feel no such transport and
rapture in loving Him as deprived those
enamoured men of their reason, and
made them unconscious of themselves."

Most of the great medieval Sūfīs lived
saintly lives, dreaming of God, intoxicated
with God. When they tried to tell their
dreams, being men, they used the language
of men. If they were also literary artists,
they naturally wrote in the style of their own
day and generation. In mystical poetry the
Arabs yield the palm to the Persians. Any
one who would read the secret of Sūfism, no
longer encumbered with theological articles
nor obscured by metaphysical subtleties—
let him turn to ʿAttār, Jalāluddīn Rūmī, and
Jāmī, whose works are partially accessible
in English and other European languages.
To translate these wonderful hymns is to
break their melody and bring their soaring
passion down to earth, but not even a prose
translation can quite conceal the love of
Truth and the vision of Beauty which inspired them. Listen again to Jalāluddīn :

" He comes, a moon whose like the sky ne'er saw,
    awake or dreaming,
  Crowned with eternal flame no flood can lay.
  Lo, from the flagon of Thy love, O Lord, my soul is
    swimming,
  And ruined all my body's house of clay.

When first the Giver of the grape my lonely heart
 befriended,
Wine fired my bosom and my veins filled up,
But when His image all mine eye possessed, a voice
 descended,
'Well done, O sovereign Wine and peerless Cup!'"

The love thus symbolised is the emotional
element in religion, the rapture of the seer,
the courage of the martyr, the faith of the
saint, the only basis of moral perfection and
spiritual knowledge. Practically, it is self-
renunciation and self-sacrifice, the giving up
of all possessions—wealth, honour, will, life,
and whatever else men value—for the Beloved's sake without any thought of reward.
I have already referred to love as the supreme
principle in Sūfī ethics, and now let me give
some illustrations.

  "Love," says Jalāluddīn, "is the
remedy of our pride and self-conceit,
the physician of all our infirmities.
Only he whose garment is rent by love
becomes entirely unselfish."

Nūrī, Raqqām, and other Sūfīs were
accused of heresy and sentenced to death.

  "When the executioner approached
Raqqām, Nūrī rose and offered himself
in his friend's place with the utmost
cheerfulness and submission. All the
spectators were astounded. The executioner said, 'Young man, the sword
is not a thing that people are so eager to

meet ; and your turn has not yet
arrived.' Nūrī answered, 'My religion
is founded on unselfishness. Life is the
most precious thing in the world : I
wish to sacrifice for my brethren's sake
the few moments which remain.' "

On another occasion Nūrī was overheard
praying as follows :

"O Lord, in Thy eternal knowledge
and power and will Thou dost punish
the people of Hell whom Thou hast
created ; and if it be Thy inexorable
will to make Hell full of mankind, Thou
art able to fill it with me alone, and to
send them to Paradise."

In proportion as the Sūfī loves God, he sees
God in all His creatures, and goes forth to
them in acts of charity. Pious works are
naught without love.

"Cheer one sad heart: thy loving deed will be
More than a thousand temples raised by thee.
One freeman whom thy kindness hath enslaved
Outweighs by far a thousand slaves set free."

The Moslem *Legend of the Saints* abounds in
tales of pity shown to animals (including the
despised dog), birds, and even insects. It is related that Bāyazīd purchased some cardamom
seed at Hamadhān, and before departing put
into his gaberdine a small quantity which
was left over. On reaching Bistām and recollecting what he had done, he took out the

seed and found that it contained a number of
ants. Saying, " I have carried the poor
creatures away from their home," he immediately set off and journeyed back to Hamadhān
—a distance of several hundred miles.

This universal charity is one of the fruits
of pantheism. The ascetic view of the world
which prevailed amongst the early Sūfīs, and
their vivid consciousness of God as a transcendent Personality rather than as an immanent Spirit, caused them to crush their
human affections relentlessly. Here is a short
story from the life of Fudayl ibn 'Iyād. It
would be touching if it were not so edifying.

> " One day he had in his lap a child
> four years old, and chanced to give it a
> kiss, as is the way of fathers. The child
> said, ' Father, do you love me ? ' ' Yes,'
> said Fudayl. ' Do you love God ? '
> ' Yes.' ' How many hearts have you ? '
> ' One.' ' Then,' asked the child, ' how
> can you love two with one heart ? '
> Fudayl perceived that the child's words
> were a divine admonition. In his zeal
> for God he began to beat his head and
> repented of his love for the child, and
> gave his heart wholly to God."

The higher Sūfī mysticism, as represented
by Jalāluddīn Rūmī, teaches that the
phenomenal is a bridge to the Real.

> " Whether it be of this world or of that,
> Thy love will lead thee yonder at the last."

And Jāmī says, in a passage which has been translated by Professor Browne :

"Even from earthly love thy face avert not,
Since to the Real it may serve to raise thee.
Ere A, B, C are rightly apprehended,
How canst thou con the pages of thy Koran ?
A sage (so heard I), unto whom a student
Came craving counsel on the course before him,
Said, 'If thy steps be strangers to love's pathways,
Depart, learn love, and then return before me !
For, shouldst thou fear to drink wine from Form's flagon,
Thou canst not drain the draught of the Ideal.
But yet beware ! Be not by Form belated :
Strive rather with all speed the bridge to traverse.
If to the bourne thou fain wouldst bear thy baggage,
Upon the bridge let not thy footsteps linger.'"

Emerson sums up the meaning of this where he says :

"Beholding in many souls the traits of the divine beauty, and separating in each soul that which is divine from the taint which it has contracted in the world, the lover ascends to the highest beauty, to the love and knowledge of the Divinity, by steps on this ladder of created souls."

"Man's love of God," says Hujwīrī, "is a quality which manifests itself, in the heart of the pious believer, in the form of veneration and magnification, so that he seeks to satisfy his Beloved and becomes impatient and restless in his desire for vision of Him, and cannot

rest with any one except Him, and
grows familiar with the recollection of
Him, and abjures the recollection of
everything besides. Repose becomes unlawful to him, and rest flees from him.
He is cut off from all habits and associations, and renounces sensual passion, and
turns towards the court of love, and
submits to the law of love, and knows
God by His attributes of perfection."
Inevitably such a man will love his fellow-
men. Whatever cruelty they inflict upon
him, he will perceive only the chastening
hand of God, " whose bitters are very
sweets to the soul." Bāyazīd said that
when God loves a man, He endows him
with three qualities in token thereof : a
bounty like that of the sea, a sympathy like
that of the sun, and a humility like that of
the earth. No suffering can be too great,
no devotion too high, for the piercing insight and burning faith of a true lover.

Ibn al-ʿArabī claims that Islam is pecu-
liarly the religion of love, inasmuch as the
Prophet Mohammed is called God's beloved
(Habīb), but though some traces of this
doctrine occur in the Koran, its main impulse
was unquestionably derived from Christianity. While the oldest Sūfī literature, which
is written in Arabic and unfortunately has
come down to us in a fragmentary state, is
still dominated by the Koranic insistence

on fear of Allah, it also bears conspicuous
marks of the opposing Christian tradition.
As in Christianity, through Dionysius and
other writers of the Neoplatonic school, so
in Islam, and probably under the same influence, the devotional and mystical love of
God soon developed into ecstasy and enthusiasm which finds in the sensuous imagery
of human love the most suggestive medium
for its expression. Dr. Inge observes that
the Sūfīs "appear, like true Asiatics, to
have attempted to give a sacramental and
symbolic character to the indulgence of
their passions." I need not again point out
that such a view of genuine Sūfism is both
superficial and incorrect.

Love, like gnosis, is in its essence a divine
gift, not anything that can be acquired. " If
the whole world wished to attract love, they
could not; and if they made the utmost
efforts to repel it, they could not." Those
who love God are those whom God loves.
"I fancied that I loved Him," said Bāyazīd,
" but on consideration I saw that His love
preceded mine." Junayd defined love as
the substitution of the qualities of the
Beloved for the qualities of the lover. In
other words, love signifies the passing-
away of the individual self; it is an un-
controllable rapture, a God-sent grace which
must be sought by ardent prayer and
aspiration.

"O Thou in whose bat well-curved my heart like a ball
    is laid,
Nor ever a hairbreadth swerved from Thy bidding nor
    disobeyed,
I have washed mine outward clean, the water I drew
    and poured ;
Mine inward is Thy demesne — do Thou keep it
    stainless, Lord!"

Jalāluddīn teaches that man's love is really the effect of God's love by means of an apologue. One night a certain devotee was praying aloud, when Satan appeared to him and said:

"How long wilt thou cry, 'O Allah'? Be quiet, for thou wilt get no answer." The devotee hung his head in silence. After a little while he had a vision of the prophet Khadir, who said to him, "Ah, why hast thou ceased to call on God?" "Because the answer 'Here am I' came not," he replied. Khadir said, "God hath ordered me to go to thee and say this:

"'Was it not I that summoned thee to service?
Did not I make thee busy with My name?
Thy calling "Allah!" *was* My "Here am I,"
Thy yearning pain My messenger to thee.
Of all those tears and cries and supplications
I was the magnet, and I gave them wings.'"

Divine love is beyond description, yet its signs are manifest. Sarī al-Saqatī questioned Junayd concerning the nature of love.

" Some say," he answered, "that it
is a state of concord, and some say that
it is altruism, and some say that it is
so-and-so." Sarī took hold of the skin
on his forearm and pulled it, but it
would not stretch ; then he said, " I
swear by the glory of God, were I to say
that this skin hath shrivelled on this
bone for love of Him, I should be tell-
ing the truth." Thereupon he fainted
away, and his face became like a shining
moon.

Love,' the astrolabe of heavenly mysteries,'
inspires all religion worthy of the name, and
brings with it, not reasoned belief, but the
intense conviction arising from immediate
intuition. This inner light is its own evidence; he who sees it has real knowledge,
and nothing can increase or diminish his
certainty. Hence the Sūfīs never weary of
exposing the futility of a faith which supports itself on intellectual proofs, external
authority, self-interest, or self-regard of any
kind. The barren dialectic of the theologian ;
the canting righteousness of the Pharisee
rooted in forms and ceremonies ; the less
crude but equally undisinterested worship
of which the motive is desire to gain everlasting happiness in the life hereafter ;
the relatively pure devotion of the mystic
who, although he loves God, yet thinks of
himself as loving, and whose heart is not

wholly emptied of 'otherness'—all these are 'veils' to be removed.

A few sayings by those who know will be more instructive than further explanation.

"O God! whatever share of this world Thou hast allotted to me, bestow it on Thine enemies; and whatever share of the next world Thou hast allotted to me, bestow it on Thy friends. Thou art enough for me." (RĀBI'A.)

"O God! if I worship Thee in fear of Hell, burn me in Hell; and if I worship Thee in hope of Paradise, exclude me from Paradise; but if I worship Thee for Thine own sake, withhold not Thine everlasting beauty!" (RĀBI'A.)

"Notwithstanding that the lovers of God are separated from Him by their love, they have the essential thing, for whether they sleep or wake, they seek and are sought, and are not occupied with their own seeking and loving, but are enraptured in contemplation of the Beloved. It is a crime in the lover to regard his love, and an outrage in love to look at one's own seeking while one is face to face with the Sought." (BĀYAZĪD.)

"His love entered and removed all besides Him and left no trace of anything else, so that it remained single even as He is single." (BĀYAZĪD.)

" To feel at one with God for a moment is better than all men's acts of worship from the beginning to the end of the world." (SHIBLĪ.)

" Fear of the Fire, in comparison with fear of being parted from the Beloved, is like a drop of water cast into the mightiest ocean." (DHU 'L-NŪN.)

" Unless I have the face of my heart towards Thee,
I deem prayer unworthy to be reckoned as prayer.
If I turn my face to the Ka'ba, 'tis for love of Thine ;
Otherwise I am quit both of prayer and Ka'ba."
                              (JALĀLUDDĪN RŪMĪ.)

Love, again, is the divine instinct of the soul impelling it to realise its nature and destiny. The soul is the first-born of God : before the creation of the universe it lived and moved and had its being in Him, and during its earthly manifestation it is a stranger in exile, ever pining to return to its home.

" This is Love : to fly heavenward,
    To rend, every instant, a hundred veils ;
    The first moment, to renounce life ;
    The last step, to fare without feet ;
    To regard this world as invisible,
    Not to see what appears to one's self."

All the love-romances and allegories of Sūfī poetry—the tales of Laylā and Majnūn, Yūsuf (Joseph) and Zulaykhā, Salāmān and Absāl, the Moth and the Candle, the Nightingale and the Rose—are shadow-pictures of the soul's passionate longing to be re-united with God. It is impossible, in the brief space at my command, to give the reader more than a passing glimpse of the treasures which the exuberant fancy of the East has heaped together in every room of this enchanted palace. The soul is likened to a moaning dove that has lost her mate ; to a reed torn from its bed and made into a flute whose plaintive music fills the eye with tears ; to a falcon summoned by the fowler's whistle to perch again upon his wrist ; to snow melting in the sun and mounting as vapour to the sky ; to a frenzied camel swiftly plunging through the desert by night ; to a caged parrot, a fish on dry land, a pawn that seeks to become a king.

These figures imply that God is conceived as transcendent, and that the soul cannot reach Him without taking what Plotinus in a splendid phrase calls " the flight of the Alone to the Alone." Jalāluddīn says :

"The motion of every atom is towards its origin ;
A man comes to be the thing on which he is bent.
By the attraction of fondness and yearning, the soul and the heart
Assume the qualities of the Beloved, who is the Soul of souls."

' A man comes to be the thing on which he is bent ' : what, then, does the Sūfī become ? Eckhart in one of his sermons quotes the saying of St. Augustine that Man *is* what he loves, and adds this comment:

> " If he loves a stone, he is a stone ; if he loves a man, he is a man; if he loves God—I dare not say more, for if I said that he would then be God, ye might stone me."

The Moslem mystics enjoyed greater freedom of speech than their Christian brethren who owed allegiance to the medieval Catholic Church, and if they went too far the plea of ecstasy was generally accepted as a sufficient excuse. Whether they emphasise the outward or the inward aspect of unification, the transcendence or the immanence of God, their expressions are bold and uncompromising. Thus Abū Saʿīd :

> "In my heart Thou dwellest — else with blood I'll drench it ;
> In mine eye Thou glowest — else with tears I'll quench it.
> Only to be one with Thee my soul desireth—
> Else from out my body, by hook or crook, I'll wrench it ! "

Jalāluddīn Rūmī proclaims that the soul's love of God is God's love of the soul, and that in loving the soul God loves Himself, for He draws home to Himself that which in its essence is divine.

" Our copper," says the poet, " has been transmuted by this rare alchemy,"

meaning that the base alloy of self has
been purified and spiritualised.   In another
ode he says :

> "O my soul, I searched from end to end : I saw in
>   thee naught save the Beloved ;
>   Call me not infidel, O my soul, if I say that thou
>   thyself art He."

And yet more plainly :

> "Ye who in search of God, of God, pursue,
>   Ye need not search for God is you, is you !
>   Why seek ye something that was missing ne'er ?
>   Save you none is, but you are—where, oh, where ?"

Where is the lover when the Beloved has
displayed Himself ?   Nowhere and everywhere : his individuality has passed away
from him.   In the bridal chamber of Unity
God celebrates the mystical marriage of the
soul.

CHAPTER V

SAINTS AND MIRACLES

LET us suppose that the average Moslem could read English, and that we placed in his hands one of those admirable volumes published by the Society for Psychical Research. In order to sympathise with his feelings on such an occasion, we have only to imagine what our own would be if a scientific friend invited us to study a treatise setting forth the evidence in favour of telegraphy and recording well-attested instances of telegraphic communication. The Moslem would probably see in the telegraph some kind of spirit—an *afreet* or *jinnī*. Telepathy and similar occult phenomena he takes for granted as self-evident facts. It would never occur to him to investigate them. There is something in the constitution of his mind that makes it impervious to the idea that the supernatural may be subject to law. He believes, because he cannot help believing, in the reality of an unseen world which ' lies about us,' not in our infancy alone, but always and every-

where ; a world from which we are in
no wise excluded, accessible and in some
measure revealed to all, though free and open
intercourse with it is a privilege enjoyed by
few.   Many are called but few chosen.

"Spirits every night from the body's snare
   Thou freest, and makest the tablets clean.[1]
   Spirits are set free every night from this cage,
   Independent, neither ruled nor ruling.
   At night prisoners forget their prison,
   At night kings forget their power:
   No sorrow, no brooding over gain and loss,
   No thought of this person or that person.
   This is the state of the gnostic, even when he is
      awake;
   God hath said, ' Thou wouldst deem them awake while
      they slept.' [2]
   He is asleep, day and night, to the affairs of the
      world,
   Like a pen in the controlling hand of the Lord."

The Sūfīs have always declared and believed themselves to be God's chosen people.
The Koran refers in several places to His
elect.   According to the author of the *Kitāb
al-Luma'*, this title belongs, firstly, to the
prophets, elect in virtue of their sinlessness,
their inspiration, and their apostolic mission ;
and secondly, to certain Moslems, elect in
virtue of their sincere devotion and self-
mortification and firm attachment to the

---

[1] By erasing all the sensuous impressions which form a
veil between the soul and the world of reality.
[2] Kor. 18. 17.

eternal realities : in a word, the saints.
While the Sūfīs are the elect of the
Moslem community, the saints are the elect
of the Sūfīs.

The Mohammedan saint is commonly
known as a *walī* (plural, *awliyā*). This
word is used in various senses derived from
its root-meaning of ' nearness ' ; *e.g.* next
of kin, patron, protector, friend. It is applied in the Koran to God as the protector
of the Faithful, to angels or idols who are
supposed to protect their worshippers, and
to men who are regarded as being specially
under divine protection. Mohammed twits
the Jews with professing to be *protégés* of
God (*awliyā lillāh*). Notwithstanding its
somewhat equivocal associations, the term
was taken over by the Sūfīs and became the
ordinary designation of persons whose holiness brings them near to God, and who
receive from Him, as tokens of His peculiar
favour, miraculous gifts (*karāmāt, χαρίσματα*) ;
they are His friends, on whom " no fear shall
come and they shall not grieve " ; [1]   any
injury done to them is an act of hostility
against Him.

The inspiration of the Islamic saints,
though verbally distinguished from that of
the prophets and inferior in degree, is of the
same kind. In consequence of their intimate
relation to God, the veil shrouding the

[1] Kor. 10. 63.

supernatural, or, as a Moslem would say, the unseen world, from their perceptions is withdrawn at intervals, and in their fits of ecstasy they rise to the prophetic level. Neither deep learning in divinity, nor devotion to good works, nor asceticism, nor moral purity makes the Mohammedan a saint ; he may have all or none of these things, but the only indispensable qualification is that ecstasy and rapture which is the outward sign of ' passing-away ' from the phenomenal self. Any one thus enraptured (*majdhūb*) is a *walī*,[1] and when such persons are recognised through their power of working miracles, they are venerated as saints not only after death but also during their lives. Often, however, they live and die in obscurity. Hujwīrī tells us that amongst the saints " there are four thousand who are concealed and do not know one another and are not aware of the excellence of their state, being in all circumstances hidden from themselves and from mankind."

The saints form an invisible hierarchy, on which the order of the world is thought to depend. Its supreme head is entitled the *Quṭb* (Axis). He is the most eminent Sūfī of his age, and presides over the meetings regularly held by this august parliament, whose members are not hampered in their attendance by the inconvenient fictions of

[1] *Waliyyat*, if the saint is a woman.

time and space, but come together from all
parts of the earth in the twinkling of an eye,
traversing seas and mountains and deserts
as easily as common mortals step across a
road.   Below the *Qutb* stand various classes
and grades of sanctity.   Hujwīrī enumerates
them, in ascending series, as follows : three
hundred *Akhyār* (Good), forty *Abdāl*
(Substitutes), seven *Abrār* (Pious), four
Awtād (Supports), and three *Nuqabā* (Over-
seers).

> " All these know one another and
> cannot act save by mutual consent.   It
> is the task of the *Awtād* to go round the
> whole world every night, and if there
> should be any place on which their eyes
> have not fallen, next day some flaw
> will appear in that place, and they must
> then inform the *Qutb* in order that he
> may direct his attention to the weak
> spot and that by his blessing the im-
> perfection may be remedied."

We are studying in this book the mystical
life of the individual Moslem, and it is
necessary to keep the subject within the
narrowest bounds.   Otherwise, I should have
liked to dwell on the external and historical
organisation of Sūfism as a school for saints,
and to describe the process of evolution
through which the *walī* privately conversing
with a small circle of friends became, first,
a teacher and spiritual guide gathering

disciples around him during his lifetime, and finally the head of a perpetual religious order which bore his name. The earliest of these great fraternities date from the twelfth century. In addition to their own members—the so-called ' dervishes '—each order has a large number of lay brethren attached to it, so that their influence pervades all ranks of Moslem society. They are " independent and self - developing. There is rivalry between them ; but no one rules over the other. In faith and practice each goes its own way, limited only by the universal conscience of Islam. Thus strange doctrines and grave moral defects easily develop unheeded, but freedom is saved." [1] Of course, the typical *walī* is incapable of founding an order, but Islam has produced no less frequently than Christendom men who combine intense spiritual illumination with creative energy and aptitude for affairs on a grand scale. The Mohammedan notion of the saint as a person possessed by God allows a very wide application of the term : in popular usage it extends from the greatest Sūfī theosophists, like Jalāluddīn Rūmī and Ibn al-'Arabī, down to those who have gained sanctity only by losing sanity— victims of epilepsy and hysteria, half-witted idiots and harmless lunatics.

[1] D. B. Macdonald, *The Religious Life and Attitude in Islam*, p. 164.

Both Qushayrī [1] and Hujwīrī discuss the question whether a saint can be conscious of his saintship, and answer it in the affirmative. Their opponents argue that consciousness of saintship involves assurance of salvation, which is impossible, since no one can know with certainty that he shall be among the saved on the Day of Judgment. In reply it was urged that God may miraculously assure the saint of his predestined salvation, while maintaining him in a state of spiritual soundness and preserving him from disobedience. The saint is not immaculate, as the prophets are, but the divine protection which he enjoys is a guarantee that he will not persevere in evil courses, though he may temporarily be led astray. According to the view generally held, saintship depends on faith, not on conduct, so that no sin except infidelity can cause it to be forfeited. This perilous theory, which opens the door to antinomianism, was mitigated by the emphasis laid on fulfilment of the religious law. The following anecdote of Bāyazīd. al-Bistāmī shows the official attitude of all the leading Sūfīs who are cited as authorities in the Moslem text-books.

" I was told (he said) that a saint of God was living in such-and-such a town,

[1] Author of a famous work designed to close the breach between Sūfism and Islam. He died in 1074 A.D.

and I set out to visit him. When I entered the mosque, he came forth from his chamber and spat on the floor. I turned back without saluting him, saying to myself, ' A saint must keep the religious law in order that God may keep him in his spiritual state. Had this man been a saint, his respect for the law would have prevented him from spitting on the floor, or God would have saved him from marring the grace vouchsafed to him."

Many *walīs*, however, regard the law as a curb that is indeed necessary so long as one remains in the disciplinary stage, but may be discarded by the saint. Such a person, they declare, stands on a higher plane than ordinary men, and is not to be condemned for actions which outwardly seem irreligious. While the older Sūfīs insist that a *walī* who breaks the law is thereby shown to be an impostor, the popular belief in the saints and the rapid growth of saint-worship tended to aggrandise the *walī* at the expense of the law, and to foster the conviction that a divinely gifted man can do no wrong, or at least that his actions must not be judged by appearances. The classical instance of this *jus divinum* vested in the friends of God is the story of Moses and Khadir, which is related in the Koran (18. 64–80). Khadir or Khizr —the Koran does not mention him by name

—is a mysterious sage endowed with immortality, who is said to enter into conversation with wandering Sūfīs and impart to them his God-given knowledge. Moses desired to accompany him on a journey that he might profit by his teaching, and Khadir consented, only stipulating that Moses should ask no questions of him.

" So they both went on, till they embarked in a boat and he (Khadir) staved it in. ' What ! ' cried Moses, ' hast thou staved it in that thou mayst drown its crew ? Verily, a strange thing hast thou done.'

" He said, ' Did not I tell thee that thou couldst no way have patience with me ? '

" Then they went on until they met a youth, and he slew him. Said Moses, ' Hast thou slain him who is free from guilt of blood ? Surely now thou hast wrought an unheard-of thing ! ' "

After Moses had broken his promise of silence for the third time, Khadir resolved to leave him.

" But first," he said, " I will tell thee the meaning of that with which thou couldst not have patience. As to the boat, it belonged to poor men, toilers on the sea, and I was minded to damage it, for in their rear was a king who seized on every boat by force. And as to the youth, his parents were believers, and I feared lest he should trouble them by error and unbelief."

The Sūfīs are fond of quoting this unimpeachable testimony that the *walī* is above human criticism, and that his hand, as Jalāluddīn asserts, is even as the hand of God. Most Moslems admit the claim to be valid in so far as they shrink from applying conventional standards of morality to holy men. I have explained its metaphysical justification in an earlier chapter.

A miracle performed by a saint is termed *karāmat*, i.e. a ' favour ' which God bestows upon him, whereas a miracle performed by a prophet is called *mu'jizat*, i.e. an act which cannot be imitated by any one. The distinction originated in controversy, and was used to answer those who held the miraculous powers of the saints to be a grave encroachment on the prerogative of the Prophet. Sūfī apologists, while confessing that both kinds of miracle are substantially the same, take pains to differentiate the characteristics of each ; they declare, moreover, that the saints are the Prophet's witnesses, and that all their miracles (like ' a drop trickling from a full skin of honey ') are in reality derived from him. This is the orthodox view and is supported by those Mohammedan mystics who acknowledge the Law as well

as the Truth, though in some cases it may
have amounted to little more than a pious
opinion. We have often noticed the difficulty in which the Sūfīs find themselves when
they try to make a logical compromise with
Islam. But the word ' logic ' is very mis-
leading in this connexion. The beginning
of wisdom, for European students of Oriental
religion, lies in the discovery that incon-
gruous beliefs—I mean, of course, beliefs
which *our* minds cannot harmonise—dwell
peacefully together in the Oriental brain ;
that their owner is quite unconscious of
their incongruity ; and that, as a rule, he
is absolutely sincere. Contradictions which
seem glaring to us do not trouble him at all.

The thaumaturgic element in ancient
Sūfism was not so important as it afterwards
became in the fully developed saint-worship
associated with the Dervish Orders. " A
saint would be none the less a saint," says
Qushayrī, " if no miracles were wrought by
him in this world." In early Mohammedan
Vitæ Sanctorum it is not uncommon to
meet with sayings to the effect that miraculous powers are comparatively of small
account. It was finely said by Sahl ibn
'Abdallah that the greatest miracle is the
substitution of a good quality for a bad
one ; and the *Kitāb al-Luma'* gives many
examples of holy men who disliked miracles and regarded them as a temptation.

"During my novitiate," said Bāyazīd,
"God used to bring before me wonders and
miracles, but I paid no heed to them ; and
when He saw that I did so, He gave me the
means of attaining to knowledge of Himself."
Junayd observed that reliance on miracles
is one of the ' veils ' which hinder the elect
from penetrating to the inmost shrine of the
Truth. This was too high doctrine for the
great mass of Moslems, and in the end
the vulgar idea of saintship triumphed
over the mystical and theosophical conception. All such warnings and scruples
were swept aside by the same irresistible
instinct which rendered vain the solemn
asseverations of Mohammed that there was
nothing supernatural about him, and which
transformed the human Prophet of history
into an omnipotent hierophant and magician.
The popular demand for miracles far ex-
ceeded the supply, but where the *walīs*
failed, a vivid and credulous imagination
came to their rescue and represented them,
not as they were, but as they ought to be.
Year by year the *Legend of the Saints*
grew more glorious and wonderful as it
continued to draw fresh tribute from the
unfathomable ocean of Oriental romance.
The pretensions made by the *walīs*, or on
their behalf, steadily increased, and the
stories told of them were ever becoming more
fantastic and extravagant. I will devote

the remainder of this chapter to a sketch
of the *walī* as he appears in the vast medieval
literature on the subject.

The Moslem saint does not say that he has
wrought a miracle ; he says, " a miracle was
granted or manifested to me." According
to one view, he may be fully conscious at
the time, but many Sūfīs hold that such
' manifestation ' cannot take place except
in ecstasy, when the saint is entirely under
divine control. His own personality is then
in abeyance, and those who interfere with
him oppose the Almighty Power which speaks
with his lips and smites with his hand.
Jalāluddīn (who uses incidentally the rather
double-edged analogy of a man possessed
by a peri[1]) relates the following anecdote
concerning Bāyazīd of Bistām, a celebrated
Persian saint who several times declared
in ecstatic frenzy that he was no other than
God.

After coming to himself on one of these
occasions and learning what blasphemous
language he had uttered, Bāyazīd ordered
his disciples to stab him with their knives
if he should offend again. Let me quote
the sequel, from Mr. Whinfield's abridged
translation of the *Masnavī* (p. 196) :

> "The torrent of madness bore away his reason
> And he spoke more impiously than before:
> 'Within my vesture is naught but God,

---

[1] One of the spirits called collectively Jinn.

Whether you seek Him on earth or in heaven.'
His disciples all became mad with horror,
And struck with their knives at his holy body.
Each one who aimed at the body of the Sheykh—
His stroke was reversed and wounded the striker.
No stroke took effect on that man of spiritual gifts,
But the disciples were wounded and drowned in blood."

Here is the poet's conclusion :

"Ah! you who smite with your sword him beside
        himself,
You smite yourself therewith.   Beware!
For he that is beside himself is annihilated and safe;
Yea, he dwells in security for ever.
His form is vanished, he is a mere mirror;
Nothing is seen in him but the reflexion of another.
If you spit at it, you spit at your own face,
And if you hit that mirror, you hit yourself.
If you see an ugly face in it, 'tis your own,
And if you see a Jesus there, you are its mother
        Mary.
He is neither this nor that—he is void of form;
'Tis your own form which is reflected back to you."

The life of Abu 'l-Hasan Khurqānī, another Persian Sūfī who died in 1033 A.D., gives us a complete picture of the Oriental pantheist, and exhibits the mingled arrogance and sublimity of the character as clearly as could be desired. Since the original text covers fifty pages, I can translate only a small portion of it here.

"Once the Sheykh said, ' This night a great many persons (he mentioned the exact number) have been wounded by brigands in such-and-such a desert.'

On making inquiry, they found that
his statement was perfectly true.
Strange to relate, on the same night
his son's head was cut off and laid upon
the threshold of his house, yet he knew
nothing of it. His wife, who disbelieved
in him, cried, ' What think you of a
man who can tell things which happen
many leagues away, but does not know
that his own son's head has been cut
off and is lying at his very door ? '
' Yes,' the Sheykh answered, ' when I
saw that, the veil had been lifted, but
when my son was killed, it had been let
down again.' "

    " One day Abu 'l-Hasan Khurqānī
clenched his fist and extended the little
finger and said, ' Here is the *qibla*,[1] if any
one desires to become a Sūfī.' These
words were reported to the Grand
Sheykh, who, deeming the co-existence
of two *qiblas* an insult to the divine
Unity, exclaimed, ' Since a second *qibla*
has appeared, I will cancel the former
one.' After that, no pilgrims were able to
reach Mecca. Some perished on the way,
others fell into the hands of robbers,
or were prevented by various causes
from accomplishing their journey. Next
year a certain dervish said to the Grand

[1] The *qibla* is the point to which Moslems turn their faces
when praying, *i.e.* the Ka'ba.

Sheykh, ' What sense is there in keeping the folk away from the House of God ? ' Thereupon the Grand Sheykh made a sign, and the road became open once more. The dervish asked, ' Whose fault is it that all these people have perished ? ' The Grand Sheykh replied, ' When elephants jostle each other, who cares if a few wretched birds are crushed to death ? ' ' "

" Some persons who were setting forth on a journey begged Khurqānī to teach them a prayer that would keep them safe from the perils of the road. He said, ' If any misfortune should befall you, mention my name.' This answer was not agreeable to them ; they set off, however, and while travelling were attacked by brigands. One of the party mentioned the saint's name and immediately became invisible, to the great astonishment of the brigands, who could not find either his camel or his bales of merchandise ; the others lost all their clothes and goods. On returning home, they asked the Sheykh to explain the mystery. ' We all invoked God,' they said, ' and without success ; but the one man who invoked you vanished from before the eyes of the robbers.' ' You invoke God formally,' said the Sheykh, ' whereas

I invoke Him really. Hence, if you invoke me and I then invoke God on your behalf, your prayers are granted ; but it is useless for you to invoke God formally and by rote.' "

"One night, while he was praying, he heard a voice cry, 'Ha! Abu 'l-Hasan! Dost thou wish Me to tell the people what I know of thee, that they may stone thee to death ?' 'O Lord God,' he replied, ' dost Thou wish me to tell the people what I know of Thy mercy and what I perceive of Thy grace, that none of them may ever again bow to Thee in prayer ?' The voice answered, ' Keep thy secret, and I will keep Mine.' "

" He said, ' O God, do not send to me the Angel of Death, for I will not give up my soul to him. How should I restore it to him, from whom I did not receive it ? I received my soul from Thee, and I will not give it up to any one but Thee.' "

" He said, ' After I shall have passed away, the Angel of Death will come to one of my descendants and set about taking his soul, and will deal hardly with him. Then will I raise my hands from the tomb and shed the grace of God upon his lips.' "

" He said, ' If I bade the empyrean

move, it would obey, and if I told the
sun to stop, it would cease from rolling
on its course.' "

"He said, ' I am not a devotee nor
an ascetic nor a theologian nor a Sūfī.
O God, Thou art One, and through Thy
Oneness I am One.' "

" He said, ' The skull of my head is
the empyrean, and my feet are under
the earth, and my two hands are East
and West.' "

" He said, ' If any one does not
believe that I shall stand up at the
Resurrection and that he shall not
enter Paradise until I lead him forward, let him not come here to salute
me.' "

" He said, ' Since God brought me
forth from myself, Paradise is in quest
of me and Hell is in fear of me ; and
if Paradise and Hell were to pass by
this place where I am, both would
become annihilated in me, together with
all the people whom they contain.' "

" He said, ' I was lying on my back,
asleep. From a corner of the Throne
of God something trickled into my
mouth, and I felt a sweetness in my
inward being.' "

" He said, ' If a few drops of that
which is under the skin of a saint
should come forth between his lips,

all the creatures of heaven and earth
would fall into panic.' "

" He said, ' Through prayer the saints
are able to stop the fish from swim-
ming in the sea and to make the earth
tremble, so that people think it is an
earthquake.' "

" He said, ' If the love of God in
the hearts of His friends were made
manifest, it would fill the world with
flood and fire.' "

" He said, ' He that lives with God
hath seen all things visible, and heard
all things audible, and done all that is
to be done, and known all that is to
be known.' "

" He said, ' All things are contained
in me, but there is no room for myself
in me.' "

" He said, ' Miracles are only the
first of the thousand stages of the Way
to God.' "

" He said, ' Do not seek until thou
art sought, for when thou findest that
which thou seekest, it will resemble
thee.' "

" He said, ' Thou must daily die a
thousand deaths and come to life again,
that thou mayst win the life immortal.' "

" He said, ' When thou givest to
God thy nothingness, He gives to thee
His All.' "

It would be an almost endless task to enumerate and exemplify the different classes of miracles which are related in the lives of the Mohammedan saints—for instance, walking on water, flying in the air (with or without a passenger), rain-making, appearing in various places at the same time, healing by the breath, bringing the dead to life, knowledge and prediction of future events, thought-reading, telekinesis, paralysing or beheading an obnoxious person by a word or gesture, conversing with animals or plants, turning earth into gold or precious stones, producing food and drink, etc. To the Moslem, who has no sense of natural law, all these ' violations of custom,' as he calls them, seem equally credible. We, on the other hand, feel ourselves obliged to distinguish phenomena which we regard as irrational and impossible from those for which we can find some sort of ' natural ' explanation. Modern theories of psychical influence, faith-healing, telepathy, veridical hallucination, hypnotic suggestion and the like, have thrown open to us a wide avenue of approach to this dark continent in the Eastern mind. I will not, however, pursue the subject far at present, full of interest as it is. In the higher Sūfī teaching the miraculous powers of the saints play a more or less insignificant part, and the excessive importance which they assume in the organ-

ised mysticism of the Dervish Orders is one
of the clearest marks of its degeneracy.

The following passage, which I have
slightly modified, gives a fair summary of
the hypnotic process through which a dervish
attains to union with God :

" The disciple must, mystically,
always bear his Murshid (spiritual
director) in mind, and become mentally
absorbed in him through a constant
meditation and contemplation of him.
The teacher must be his shield against
all evil thoughts. The spirit of the
teacher follows him in all his efforts, and
accompanies him wherever he may be,
quite as a guardian spirit. To such a
degree is this carried that he sees the
master in all men and in all things, just
as a willing subject is under the influence
of the magnetiser. This condition is
called ' self-annihilation ' in the Murshid
or Sheykh. The latter finds, in his own
visionary dreams, the degree which the
disciple has reached, and whether or
not his spirit has become bound to his
own.

" At this stage the Sheykh passes him
over to the spiritual influence of the
long-deceased Pīr or original founder of
the Order, and he sees the latter only by
the spiritual aid of the Sheykh. This is
called ' self-annihilation ' in the Pīr. He

now becomes so much a part of the Pīr as to possess all his spiritual powers.

" The third grade leads him, also through the spiritual aid of the Sheykh, up to the Prophet himself, whom he now sees in all things. This state is called ' self-annihilation ' in the Prophet.

" The fourth degree leads him even to God. He becomes united with the Deity and sees Him in all things." [1]

An excellent concrete illustration of the process here described will be found in the well-known case of Tawakkul Beg, who passed through all these experiences under the control of Mollā-Shāh. His account is too long to quote in full; moreover, it has recently been translated by Professor D. B. Macdonald in his *Religious Life and Attitude in Islam* (pp. 197 ff.). I copy from this version one paragraph describing the first of the four stages mentioned above.

" Thereupon he made me sit before him, my senses being as though intoxicated, and ordered me to reproduce my own image within myself; and, after having bandaged my eyes, he asked me to concentrate all my mental faculties on my heart. I obeyed, and in an instant, by the divine favour and by the spiritual assistance of the Sheykh, my

[1] J. P. Brown, *The Dervishes, or Oriental Spiritualism* (1868), p. 298.

heart opened. I saw, then, that there was something like an overturned cup within me. This having been set upright, a sensation of unbounded happiness filled my being. I said to the master, ' This cell where I am seated before you—I see a faithful reproduction of it within me, and it appears to me as though another Tawakkul Beg were seated before another Mollā-Shāh.' He replied, ' Very good ! the first apparition which appears to thee is the image of the master.' He then ordered me to uncover my eyes ; and I saw him, with the physical organ of vision, seated before me. He then made me bind my eyes again, and I perceived him with my spiritual sight, seated similarly before me. Full of astonishment, I cried out, ' O Master ! whether I look with my physical organs or with my spiritual sight, always it is you that I see ! ' "

Here is a case of autohypnotism, witnessed and recorded by the poet Jāmī :

" Mawlānā Sa'duddīn of Kāshghar, after a little concentration of thought (*tawajjuh*), used to exhibit signs of unconsciousness. Any one ignorant of this circumstance would have fancied that he was falling asleep. When I first entered into companionship with him,

I happened one day to be seated before
him in the congregational mosque. According to his custom, he fell into a
trance. I supposed that he was going
to sleep, and I said to him, ' If you
desire to rest for a short time, you will
not seem to me to be far off.' He
smiled and said, ' Apparently you do
not believe that this is something
different from sleep.' "

The following anecdote presents greater
difficulties :

"Mawlānā Nizāmuddīn Khāmūsh
relates that one day his master, 'Alā-
'uddīn 'Attār, started to visit the tomb
of the celebrated saint Mohammed ibn
'Alī Hakīm, at Tirmidh. ' I did not
accompany him,' said Nizāmuddīn,
' but stayed at home, and by concen-
trating my mind (*tawajjuh*) I succeeded
in bringing the spirituality of the saint
before me, so that when the master
arrived at the tomb he found it empty.
He must have known the cause, for on
his return he set to work in order to
bring me under his control. I, too,
concentrated my mind, but I found
myself like a dove and the master like a
hawk flying in chase of me. Wherever
I turned, he was always close behind.
At last, despairing of escape, I took
refuge with the spirituality of the

Prophet (on whom be peace) and
became effaced in its infinite radiance.
The master could not exercise any
further control. He fell ill in consequence of his chagrin, and no one except
myself knew the reason.'"

'Alā'uddīn's son, Khwāja Hasan 'Attār,
possessed such powers of ' control ' that he
could at will throw any one into the state
of trance and cause them to experience
the ' passing-away ' (fanā) to which some
mystics attain only on rare occasions and
after prolonged self-mortification. It is related that the disciples and visitors who
were admitted to the honour of kissing his
hand always fell unconscious to the ground.

Certain saints are believed to have the
power of assuming whatever shape they
please. One of the most famous was Abū
'Abdallah of Mosul, better known by the
name of Qadīb al-Bān. One day the Cadi
of Mosul, who regarded him as a detestable
heretic, saw him in a street of the town,
approaching from the opposite direction.
He resolved to seize him and lay a charge
against him before the governor, in order
that he might be punished. All at once he
perceived that Qadīb al-Bān had taken the
form of a Kurd ; and as the saint advanced
towards him, his appearance changed again,
this time into an Arab of the desert. Finally,
on coming still nearer, he assumed the guise

and dress of a doctor of theology, and cried,
" O Cadi! which Qadīb al-Bān will you hale
before the governor and punish?" The
Cadi repented of his hostility and became
one of the saint's disciples.

In conclusion, let me give two alleged
instances of 'the obedience of inanimate
objects,' *i.e.* telekinesis:

" Whilst Dhu 'l-Nūn was conversing
on this topic with some friends, he
said, ' Here is a sofa. It will move
round the room, if I tell it to do so.'
No sooner had he uttered the word
' move ' than the sofa made a circuit
of the room and returned to its place.
One of the spectators, a young man,
burst into tears and gave up the ghost.
They laid him on that sofa and washed
him for burial."

" Avicenna paid a visit to Abu
'l-Hasan Khurqānī and immediately
plunged into a long and abstruse discussion. After a time the saint, who
was an illiterate person, felt tired, so
he got up and said, ' Excuse me; I
must go and mend the garden wall ';
and off he went, taking a hatchet with
him. As soon as he had climbed on to
the top of the wall, the hatchet dropped
from his hand. Avicenna ran to pick
it up, but before he reached it the
hatchet rose of itself and came back

into the saint's hand. Avicenna lost all his self-command, and the enthusiastic belief in Sūfism which then took possession of him continued until, at a later period of his life, he abandoned mysticism for philosophy."

I am well aware that in this chapter scanty justice has been done to a great subject. The historian of Sūfism must acknowledge, however deeply he may deplore, the fundamental position occupied by the doctrine of saintship and the tremendous influence which it has exerted in its practical results—grovelling submission to the authority of an ecstatic class of men, dependence on their favour, pilgrimage to their shrines, adoration of their relics, devotion of every mental and spiritual faculty to their service. It may be dangerous to worship God by one's own inner light, but it is far more deadly to seek Him by the inner light of another. Vicarious holiness has no compensations. This truth is expressed by the mystical writers in many an eloquent passage, but I will content myself with quoting a few lines from the life of 'Alā'uddīn 'Attār, the same saint who, as we have seen, vainly tried to hypnotise his pupil in revenge for a disrespectful trick which the latter had played on him. His biographer relates that he said, " It is more right and worthy to dwell beside God than to dwell beside God's creatures," and that the following verse was often on his blessed tongue :

" How long will you worship at the tombs of holy men ?
Busy yourself with the *works* of holy men, and you are saved ! "

> (" *tu tā kay gūr-i mardān-rā parastī*
> *bi-gird-i kār-i mardān gard u rastī.*")

CHAPTER VI

THE UNITIVE STATE

" The story admits of being told up to this point,
But what follows is hidden, and inexpressible in words.
If you should speak and try a hundred ways to ex-
    press it,
'Tis useless; the mystery becomes no clearer.
You can ride on saddle and horse to the sea-coast,
But then you must use a horse of wood (*i.e.* a boat).
A horse of wood is useless on dry land,
It is the special vehicle of voyagers by sea.
Silence is this horse of wood,
Silence is the guide and support of men at sea." [1]

No one can approach the subject of this chapter—the state of the mystic who has reached his journey's end—without feeling that all symbolical descriptions of union with God and theories concerning its nature are little better than leaps in the dark. How shall we form any conception of that which is declared to be ineffable by those who have actually experienced it ? I can only reply that the same difficulty confronts us in dealing with all mystical phenomena,

[1] The *Masnavī* of Jalāluddīn Rūmī. Abridged translation by E. H. Whinfield, p. 326.

though it appears less formidable at lower
levels, and that the poet's counsel of silence
has not prevented him from interpreting
the deepest mysteries of Sūfism with un-
rivalled insight and power.

Whatever terms may be used to describe
it, the unitive state is the culmination of
the simplifying process by which the soul
is gradually isolated from all that is foreign
to itself, from all that is not God. Unlike
Nirvāṇa, which is merely the cessation of
individuality, *fanā*, the passing-away of the
Sūfī from his phenomenal existence, involves
baqā, the continuance of his real existence.
He who dies to self lives in God, and
fanā, the consummation of this death, marks
the attainment of *baqā*, or union with the
divine life. Deification, in short, is the
Moslem mystic's *ultima Thule*.

In the early part of the tenth century
Husayn ibn Mansūr, known to fame as
al-Hallāj (the wool-carder), was barbarously
done to death at Baghdād. His execution
seems to have been dictated by political
motives, but with these we are not concerned.
Amongst the crowd assembled round the
scaffold, a few, perhaps, believed him to
be what he said he was; the rest witnessed
with exultation or stern approval the punishment of a blasphemous heretic. He had
uttered in two words a sentence which
Islam has, on the whole, forgiven but has

never forgotten : " *Ana 'l-Haqq* "—" I am God."

The recently published researches of M. Louis Massignon[1] make it possible, for the first time, to indicate the meaning which Hallāj himself attached to this celebrated formula, and to assert definitely that it does not agree with the more orthodox interpretations offered at a later epoch by Sūfīs belonging to various schools. According to Hallāj, man is essentially divine. God created Adam in His own image. He projected from Himself that image of His eternal love, that He might behold Himself as in a mirror. Hence He bade the angels worship Adam (Kor. 2. 32), in whom, as in Jesus, He became incarnate.

> "Glory to Him who revealed in His humanity (*i.e.* in Adam) the secret of His radiant divinity,
> And then appeared to His creatures visibly in the shape of one who ate and drank (Jesus)."

Since the ' humanity ' (*nāsūt*) of God comprises the whole bodily and spiritual nature of man, the ' divinity ' (*lāhūt*) of God cannot unite with that nature except by means of an incarnation or, to adopt the term employed by Massignon, an infusion (*hulūl*) of the divine Spirit, such as takes place when the human spirit enters the

[1] *Kitāb al-Tawāsīn* (Paris, 1913). See especially pp. 129–141.

body.[1] Thus Hallāj says in one of his poems :

> "Thy Spirit is mingled in my spirit even as wine is mingled with pure water.
> When anything touches Thee, it touches me. Lo, in every case Thou art I!"

And again :

> "I am He whom I love, and He whom I love is I:
> We are two spirits dwelling in one body.
> If thou seest me, thou seest Him,
> And if thou seest Him, thou seest us both."

This doctrine of personal deification, in the peculiar form which was impressed upon it by Hallāj, is obviously akin to the central doctrine of Christianity, and therefore, from the Moslem standpoint, a heresy of the worst kind. It survived unadulterated only amongst his immediate followers. The Hulūlīs, *i.e.* those who believe in incarnation, are repudiated by Sūfīs in general quite as vehemently as by orthodox Moslems. But while the former have unhesitatingly condemned the doctrine of *hulūl*, they have also done their best to clear Hallāj from the suspicion of having taught it. Three main lines of defence are followed : (1)

---

[1] Massignon appears to be right in identifying the Divine Spirit with the Active Reason (*intellectus agens*), which, according to Alexander of Aphrodisias, is not a part or faculty of our soul, but comes to us from without. See Inge, *Christian Mysticism*, pp. 360, 361. The doctrine of Hallāj may be compared with that of Tauler, Ruysbroeck, and others concerning the birth of God in the soul.

Hallāj did not sin against the Truth, but he was justly punished in so far as he committed a grave offence against the Law. He "betrayed the secret of his Lord" by proclaiming to all and sundry the supreme mystery which ought to be reserved for the elect. (2) Hallāj spoke under the intoxicating influence of ecstasy. He imagined himself to be united with the divine essence, when in fact he was only united with one of the divine attributes. (3) Hallāj meant to declare that there is no essential difference or separation between God and His creatures, inasmuch as the divine unity includes all being. A man who has entirely passed away from his phenomenal self exists *quâ* his real self, which is God.

> "In that glory is no 'I' or 'We' or 'Thou.'
> 'I,' 'We,' 'Thou,' and 'He' are all one thing."

It was not Hallāj who cried "*Ana 'l-Haqq*," but God Himself, speaking, as it were, by the mouth of the selfless Hallāj, just as He spoke to Moses through the medium of the burning bush (Kor. 20. 8–14). The last explanation, which converts *Ana 'l-Haqq* into an impersonal monistic axiom, is accepted by most Sūfīs as representing the true Hallājian teaching. In a magnificent ode Jalāluddīn Rūmī describes how the One Light shines in myriad forms through the whole universe, and how

the One Essence, remaining ever the same,
clothes itself from age to age in the prophets
and saints who are its witnesses to mankind.

" Every moment the robber Beauty rises in a different
    shape, ravishes the soul, and disappears.
Every instant that Loved One assumes a new garment,
    now of eld, now of youth.
Now He plunged into the heart of the substance of
    the potter's clay—the Spirit plunged, like a diver.
Anon He rose from the depths of mud that is moulded
    and baked, then He appeared in the world.
He became Noah, and at His prayer the world was
    flooded while He went into the Ark.
He became Abraham and appeared in the midst of
    the fire, which turned to roses for His sake.
For a while He was roaming on the earth to pleasure
    Himself,
Then He became Jesus and ascended to the dome of
    Heaven and began to glorify God.
In brief, it was He that was coming and going in
    every generation thou hast seen,
Until at last He appeared in the form of an Arab
    and gained the empire of the world.
What is it that is transferred? What is transmigra-
    tion in reality? The lovely winner of hearts
Became a sword and appeared in the hand of 'Alī
    and became the Slayer of the time.
No! no! for 'twas even He that was crying in human
    shape, ' Ana 'l-Haqq.'
That one who mounted the scaffold was not Mansūr,[1]
    though the foolish imagined it.
Rūmī hath not spoken and will not speak words of
    infidelity: do not disbelieve him!
Whosoever shows disbelief is an infidel and one of
    those who have been doomed to Hell."

---

[1] Hallāj is often called Mansūr, which is properly the
name of his father.

Although in Western and Central Asia—
where the Persian kings were regarded
by their subjects as gods, and where the
doctrines of incarnation, anthropomorphism,
and metempsychosis are indigenous—the
idea of the God-man was neither so un-
familiar nor unnatural as to shock the
public conscience very profoundly, Hallāj
had formulated that idea in such a way that
no mysticism calling itself Mohammedan
could tolerate, much less adopt it. To
assert that the divine and human natures
may be interfused and commingled,[1] would
have been to deny the principle of unity
on which Islam is based. The subsequent
history of Sūfism shows how deification
was identified with unification. The anti-
thesis — God, Man — melted away in the
pantheistic theory which has been explained
above.[2] There is no real existence apart
from God. Man is an emanation or a reflexion or a mode of Absolute Being. What
he thinks of as individuality is in truth not-
being ; it cannot be separated or united,
for it does not exist. Man *is* God, yet with

---

[1] *Hulūl* was not understood in this sense by Hallāj
(Massignon, *op. cit.*, p. 199), though the verses quoted on
p. 151 readily suggest such an interpretation. Hallāj, I
think, would have agreed with Eckhart (who said, " The
word *I am* none can truly speak but God alone ") that
the personality in which the Eternal is immanent has itself
a part in eternity (Inge, *Christian Mysticism*, p. 149, note).
[2] See pp. 79 ff.

a difference. According to Ibn al-'Arabī,[1] the eternal and the phenomenal are two complementary aspects of the One, each of which is necessary to the other. The creatures are the external manifestation of the Creator, and Man is God's consciousness (*sirr*) as revealed in creation. But since Man, owing to the limitations of his mind, cannot think all objects of thought simultaneously, and therefore expresses only a part of the divine consciousness, he is not entitled to say *Ana 'l-Haqq*, "I am God." He is *a* reality, but not *the* Reality. We shall see that other Sūfīs — Jalāluddīn Rūmī, for example—in their ecstatic moments, at any rate, ignore this rather subtle distinction.

The statement that in realising the non-entity of his individual self the Sūfī realises his essential oneness with God, sums up the Mohammedan theory of deification in terms with which my readers are now familiar. I will endeavour to show what more precise meaning may be assigned to it, partly in my own words and partly by means of illustrative extracts from various authors.

Several aspects of *fanā* have already been distinguished.[2] The highest of these—the passing-away in the divine essence—is fully described by Niffarī, who employs instead of *fanā* and *fānī* (self-naughted) the terms

---

[1] Massignon, *op. cit.*, p. 183. [2] See pp. 60, 61.

waqfat, signifying cessation from search, and *wāqif*, *i.e.* one who desists from seeking and passes away in the Object Sought. Here are some of the chief points that occur in the text and commentary.

Waqfat is luminous : it expels the dark thoughts of 'otherness,' just as light banishes darkness ; it changes the phenomenal values of all existent things into their real and eternal values.

Hence the *wāqif* transcends time and place. " He enters every house and it contains him not ; he drinks from every well but is not satisfied ; then he reaches Me, and I am his home, and his abode is with Me "—that is to say, he comprehends all the divine attributes and embraces all mystical experiences. He is not satisfied with the names (attributes), but seeks the Named. He contemplates the essence of God and finds it identical with his own. He does not pray. Prayer is from man to God, but in *waqfat* there is nothing but God.

The *wāqif* leaves not a rack behind him, nor any heir except God. When even the phenomenon of *waqfat* has disappeared from his consciousness, he becomes the very Light. Then his praise of God proceeds from God, and his knowledge is God's knowledge, who beholds Himself alone as He was in the beginning.

We need not expect to discover how this

essentialisation, substitution, or transmutation is effected.   It is the grand paradox of Sūfism—the *Magnum Opus* wrought somehow *in* created man by a Being whose nature is eternally devoid of the least taint of creatureliness. As I have remarked above, the change, however it may be conceived, does not involve infusion of the divine essence (*hulūl*) or identification of the divine and human natures (*ittihād*). Both these doctrines are generally condemned. Abū Nasr al-Sarrāj criticises them in two passages of his *Kitāb al-Luma'*, as follows :

"Some mystics of Baghdād have erred in their doctrine that when they pass away from their qualities they enter into the qualities of God. This leads to incarnation (*hulūl*) or to the Christian belief concerning Jesus. The doctrine in question has been attributed to some of the ancients, but its true meaning is this, that when a man goes forth from his own qualities and enters into the qualities of God, he goes forth from his own will and enters into the will of God, knowing that his will is given to him by God and that by virtue of this gift he is severed from regarding himself, so that he becomes entirely devoted to God ; and this is one of the stages of Unitarians. Those who have erred in this doctrine have failed to

observe that the qualities of God are
not God. To make God identical with
His qualities is to be guilty of infidelity,
because God does not descend into the
heart, but that which descends into
the heart is faith in God and belief in
His unity and reverence for the thought
of Him.''

In the second passage he makes use of
a similar argument in order to refute the
doctrine of *ittihād*.

" Some have abstained from food
and drink, fancying that when a man's
body is weakened it is possible that he
may lose his humanity and be invested
with the attributes of divinity. The
ignorant persons who hold this errone-
ous doctrine cannot distinguish between
humanity and the inborn qualities of
humanity. Humanity does not depart
from man any more than blackness
departs from that which is black or
whiteness from that which is white,
but the inborn qualities of humanity
are changed and transmuted by the
all-powerful radiance that is shed upon
them from the divine Realities. The
attributes of humanity are not the
essence of humanity. Those who in-
culcate the doctrine of *fanā* mean the
passing-away of regarding one's own
actions and works of devotion through

the continuance of regarding God as
the doer of these actions on behalf of
His servant."

Hujwīrī characterises as absurd the belief
that passing-away (*fanā*) signifies loss of
essence and destruction of corporeal substance, and that 'abiding' (*baqā*) indicates
the indwelling of God in man. Real passing-
away from anything, he says, implies consciousness of its imperfection and absence
of desire for it. Whoever passes away from
his own perishable will abides in the everlasting will of God, but human attributes
cannot become divine attributes or *vice
versa.*

> "The power of fire transforms to its
> own quality anything that falls into it,
> and surely the power of God's will is
> greater than that of fire ; yet fire
> affects only the quality of iron without
> changing its substance, for iron can
> never become fire."

In another part of his work Hujwīrī
defines 'union' (*jam'*) as concentration of
thought upon the desired object. Thus
Majnūn, the Orlando Furioso of Islam,
concentrated his thoughts on Laylā, so that
he saw only her in the whole world, and all
created things assumed the form of Laylā
in his eyes. Some one came to the cell of
Bāyazīd and asked, " Is Bāyazīd here ? "
He answered, " Is any one here but God ? "

The principle in all such cases, Hujwīrī adds, is the same, namely :

> " That God divides the one substance of His love and bestows a particle thereof, as a peculiar gift, upon every one of His friends in proportion to their enravishment with Him ; then he lets down upon that particle the shrouds of fleshliness and human nature and temperament and spirit, in order that by its powerful working it may transmute to its own quality all the particles that are attached to it, until the lover's clay is wholly converted into love and all his acts and looks become so many properties of love. This state is named ' union ' alike by those who regard the inward sense and the outward expression."

Then he quotes these verses of Hallāj :

> " Thy will be done, O my Lord and Master!
> Thy will be done, O my purpose and meaning !
> O essence of my being, O goal of my desire,
> O my speech and my hints and my gestures !
> O all of my all, O my hearing and my sight,
> O my whole and my element and my particles ! "

The enraptured Sūfī who has passed beyond the illusion of subject and object and broken through to the Oneness can either deny that he is anything or affirm that he is all things. As an example of ' the negative way,' take the opening lines of an ode by

Jalāluddīn which I have rendered into
verse, imitating the metrical form of the
Persian as closely as the genius of our
language will permit :

" Lo, for I to myself am unknown, now in God's name
    what must I do ?
  I adore not the Cross nor the Crescent, I am not a
    Giaour nor a Jew.
  East nor West, land nor sea is my home, I have kin
    nor with angel nor gnome,
  I am wrought not of fire nor of foam, I am shaped
    not of dust nor of dew.
  I was born not in China afar, not in Saqsīn and not
    in Bulghār ;
  Not in India, where five rivers are, nor 'Irāq nor
    Khorāsān I grew.
  Not in this world nor that world I dwell, not in
    Paradise, neither in Hell ;
  Not from Eden and Rizwān I fell, not from Adam
    my lineage I drew.
  In a place beyond uttermost Place, in a tract without
    shadow of trace,
  Soul and body transcending I live in the soul of my
    Loved One anew ! "

The following poem, also by Jalāluddīn,
expresses the positive aspect of the cosmic
consciousness :

" If there be any lover in the world, O Moslems, 'tis I.
  If there be any believer, infidel, or Christian hermit,
    'tis I.
  The wine-dregs, the cupbearer, the minstrel, the
    harp, and the music,
  The beloved, the candle, the drink and the joy of
    the drunken—'tis I.
  The two-and-seventy creeds and sects in the world

Do not really exist: I swear by God that every creed
    and sect—'tis I.
Earth and air and water and fire—knowest thou what
    they are?
Earth and air and water and fire, nay, body and soul
    too—'tis I.
Truth and falsehood, good and evil, ease and difficulty
    from first to last,
Knowledge and learning and asceticism and piety and
    faith—'tis I.
The. fire of Hell, be assured, with its flaming limbos,
Yes, and Paradise and Eden and the Houris—'tis I.
This earth and heaven with all that they hold,
Angels, Peris, Genies, and Mankind—'tis I."

What Jalāluddīn utters in a moment of
ecstatic vision Henry More describes as a
past experience:

" How lovely " (he says), " how magnificent a state is the soul of man in,
when the life of God inactuating her
shoots her along with Himself through
heaven and earth ; makes her unite
with, and after a sort feel herself
animate, the whole world. He that is
here looks upon all things as One, and
on himself, if he can then mind himself,
as a part of the Whole."

For some Sūfīs, absorption in the ecstasy
of *fanā* is the end of their pilgrimage.
Thenceforth no relation exists between them
and the world. Nothing of themselves is
left in them ; as individuals, they are dead.
Immersed in Unity, they know neither law
nor religion nor any form of phenomenal

being. But those God-intoxicated devotees who never return to sobriety have fallen short of the highest perfection. The full circle of deification must comprehend both the inward and outward aspects of Deity— the One and the Many, the Truth and the Law. It is not enough to escape from all that is creaturely, without entering into the eternal life of God the Creator as manifested in His works. To abide in God (*baqā*) after having passed-away from selfhood (*fanā*) is the mark of the Perfect Man, who not only journeys *to* God, *i.e.* passes from plurality to unity, but *in* and *with* God, *i.e.* continuing in the unitive state, he returns with God to the phenomenal world from which he set out, and manifests unity in plurality. In this descent

> " He makes the Law his upper garment
> And the mystic Path his inner garment,"

for he brings down and displays the Truth to mankind while fulfilling the duties of the religious law. Of him it may be said, in the words of a great Christian mystic :

> " He goes *towards* God by inward love, in eternal work, and he goes *in* God by his fruitive inclination, in eternal rest. And he dwells in God ; and yet he goes out towards created things in a spirit of love towards all things, in the virtues and in works of

righteousness. And this is the most exalted summit of the inner life." [1]

'Afīfuddīn Tilimsānī, in his commentary on Niffarī, describes four mystical journeys :

The *first* begins with gnosis and ends with complete passing-away (*fanā*).

The *second* begins at the moment when passing-away is succeeded by ' abiding ' (*baqā*).

He who has attained to this station journeys in the Real, by the Real, to the Real, and he then is a reality (*haqq*).[2] Thus travelling onward, he arrives at the station of the *Quṭb*,[3] which is the station of Perfect Manhood. He becomes the centre of the spiritual universe, so that every point and limit reached by individual human beings is equally distant from his station, whether they be near or far ; since all stations revolve round his, and in relation to the *Quṭb* there is no difference between nearness and farness. To one who has gained this supreme position, knowledge and gnosis and passing-away are as rivers of his ocean, whereby he replenishes whomsoever he will. He has the right to guide others to God, and seeks permission to do so from none but himself. Before the gate of Apostleship was closed,[4] he would

[1] Ruysbroeck, quoted in E. Underhill's *Introduction to Mysticism*, p. 522.

[2] See p. 155 above.   [3] See p. 123.

[4] *I.e.* before the time of Mohammed, who is the Seal of the Prophets.

have deserved the title of Apostle, but in our day his due title is Director of Souls, and he is a blessing to those who invoke his aid, because he comprehends the innate capacities of all mankind and, like a camel-driver, speeds every one to his home.

In the *third* journey this Perfect Man turns his attention to God's creatures, either as an Apostle or as a Spiritual Director (Sheykh), and reveals himself to those who would fain be released from their faculties, to each according to his degree : to the adherent of positive religion as a theologian ; to the contemplative, who has not yet enjoyed full contemplation, as a gnostic ; to the gnostic as one who has entirely passed-away from individuality (*wāqif*) ; to the *wāqif* as a *Qutb*. He is the horizon of every mystical station and transcends the furthest range of experience known to each grade of seekers.

The *fourth* journey is usually associated with physical death. The Prophet was referring to it when he cried on his deathbed, " I choose the highest companions." In this journey, to judge from the obscure verses in which 'Afīfuddīn describes it, the Perfect Man, having been invested with all the divine attributes, becomes, so to speak, the mirror which displays God to Himself.

> " When my Beloved appears,
> With what eye do I see Him ?

With His eye, not with mine,
For none sees Him except Himself."

(IBN AL-'ARABĪ.)

The light in the soul, the eye by which it sees, and the object of its vision, all are One.

We have followed the Sūfī in his quest of Reality to a point where language fails. His progress will seldom be so smooth and unbroken as it appears in these pages. The proverbial headache after intoxication supplies a parallel to the periods of intense aridity and acute suffering that sometimes fill the interval between lower and higher states of ecstasy. Descriptions of this experience—the Dark Night of the Soul, as it is called by Christian authors—may be found in almost any biography of Mohammedan saints. Thus Jāmī relates in his *Nafaḥāt al-Uns* that a certain dervish, a disciple of the famous Shihābuddīn Suhrawardī,

" Was endowed with a great ecstasy in the contemplation of Unity and in the station of passing-away (*fanā*). One day he began to weep and lament. On being asked by the Sheykh Shihābuddīn what ailed him, he answered, ' Lo, I am debarred by plurality from the vision of Unity. I am rejected, and my former state—I cannot find it ! ' The Sheykh remarked that this was the prelude to the station of 'abiding' (*baqā*), and that his present state was higher and more sublime than the one which he was in before."

Does personality survive in the ultimate union with God? If personality means a conscious existence distinct, though not separate, from God, the majority of advanced Moslem mystics say "No!" As the rain-drop absorbed in the ocean is not annihilated but ceases to exist individually, so the disembodied soul becomes indistinguishable from the universal Deity. It is true that when Sūfī writers translate mystical union into terms of love and marriage, they do not, indeed they cannot, expunge the notion of personality, but such metaphorical phrases are not necessarily inconsistent with a pantheism which excludes all difference. To be united, here and now, with the World-Soul is the utmost imaginable bliss for souls that love each other on earth.

" Happy the moment when we are seated in the Palace, thou and I,
   With two forms and with two figures but with one soul, thou and I.
   The colours of the grove and the voice of the birds will bestow immortality
   At the time when we come into the garden, thou and I.
   The stars of heaven will come to gaze upon us;
   We shall show them the Moon itself, thou and I.
   Thou and I, individuals no more, shall be mingled in ecstasy,
   Joyful and secure from foolish babble, thou and I.

All the bright-plumed birds of heaven will devour
    their hearts with envy
In the place where we shall laugh in such a fashion,
    thou and I.
This is the greatest wonder, that thou and I, sitting
    here in the same nook,
Are at this moment both in 'Irāq and Khorāsān, thou
    and I."

(JALĀLUDDĪN RŪMĪ.)

Strange as it may seem to our Western egoism, the prospect of sharing in the general, impersonal immortality of the human soul kindles in the Sūfī an enthusiasm as deep and triumphant as that of the most ardent believer in a personal life continuing beyond the grave. Jalāluddīn, after describing the evolution of man in the material world and anticipating his further growth in the spiritual universe, utters a heartfelt prayer—for what ?—for self-annihilation in the ocean of the Godhead.

" I died as mineral and became a plant,
  I died as plant and rose to animal,
  I died as animal and I was man.
  Why should I fear? When was I less by dying?
  Yet once more I shall die as man, to soar
  With angels blest; but even from angelhood
  I must pass on: all except God doth perish.
  When I have sacrificed my angel soul,
  I shall become what no mind e'er conceived.
  Oh, let me not exist! for Non-existence
  Proclaims in organ tones, 'To Him we shall return.' "

BIBLIOGRAPHY

A. General

THOLUCK, F. A. G., *Ssufismus sive Theosophia Persarum pantheistica* (Berlin, 1821).
    In Latin. Out of date in some respects, but still worth reading.

PALMER, E. H., *Oriental Mysticism* (Cambridge, 1867).
    A treatise on Persian theosophy, based on a work by Nasafī.

VON KREMER, A., *Geschichte der herrschenden Ideen des Islams* (Leipzig, 1868), pp. 52–121.
    A brilliant sketch of the origin and development of Sūfism.

GOLDZIHER, I., *Vorlesungen über den Islam* (Heidelberg, 1910), pp. 139–200.
    An account of Sūfī asceticism and mysticism by the greatest living authority on Islam.

GOLDZIHER, I., *Muhammedanische Studien* (Halle, 1888–90), Part ii., pp. 277–378.
    Gives full details concerning the worship of Moslem saints.

MACDONALD, D. B., *The Religious Life and Attitude in Islam* (Chicago, 1909).
    A valuable introduction to the study of the moderate type of Sūfism represented by

Ghazālī. The chapters on psychology are particularly helpful.

IQBAL, SHAIKH MUHAMMAD, *The Development of Metaphysics in Persia* (London, 1908), pp. 96 ff.

GIBB, E. J. W., *History of Turkish Poetry* (London, 1900–1909), vol. i. pp. 15–69.
Outlines of Persian philosophic mysticism.

BROWNE, E. G., *Literary History of Persia* (London, 1902), vol. i. pp. 416–444.

BROWN, J. P., *The Dervishes, or Oriental Spiritualism* (London, 1868).
Unscientific, but contains much interesting material.

DEPONT, O., and COPPOLANI, X., *Les Confréries religieuses musulmanes* (Algiers, 1897).
A standard work on the Dervish Orders.

B. TRANSLATIONS

HUJWĪRĪ, *Kashf al-Mahjūb*, translated by R. A. Nicholson (London, 1911).
The oldest Persian treatise on Sūfism.

'ATTĀR, *Le Manticu 'ttair ou le Langage des Oiseaux*, translated, with an essay on the philosophical and religious poetry of Persia, by Garcin de Tassy (Paris, 1864).

JALĀLUDDĪN RŪMĪ, *Masnavī*, abridged translation by E. H. Whinfield, 2nd ed. (London, 1898).
Masnavī, Book i., translated by Sir James Redhouse (London, 1881).
Masnavī, Book ii., translated with commentary by C. E. Wilson (London, 1910).

Selected Odes from the Dīvāni Shamsi Tabrīz,
Persian text with English translation, introduction, and notes by R. A. Nicholson (Cambridge, 1898).

MAHMŪD SHABISTARĪ, *Gulshani Rāz,* Persian text
with English translation, introduction, and
notes by E. H. Whinfield (London, 1880).
A versified exposition of the chief Sūfī
doctrines. It should be read by every one
who is seriously interested in the subject.

JĀMĪ, *Lawā'ih,* Persian text with translation by
E. H. Whinfield and Mīrzā Muhammad
Kazvīnī (London, 1906).
A prose treatise on Sūfī theosophy.
Yūsuf and Zulaikha, translated into verse
by R. T. H. Griffith (London, 1882).
One of the most famous mystical love-
romances in Persian literature.

IBN AL-'ARABĪ, *Tarjumān al-Ashwāq,* a collection
of mystical odes. Arabic text with translation and commentary by R. A. Nicholson
(London, 1911).

INDEX

(Titles of books, as well as Arabic and Persian technical terms, are printed in italics.)